By buying this book you are directly supporting the mission of Green Card Voices.

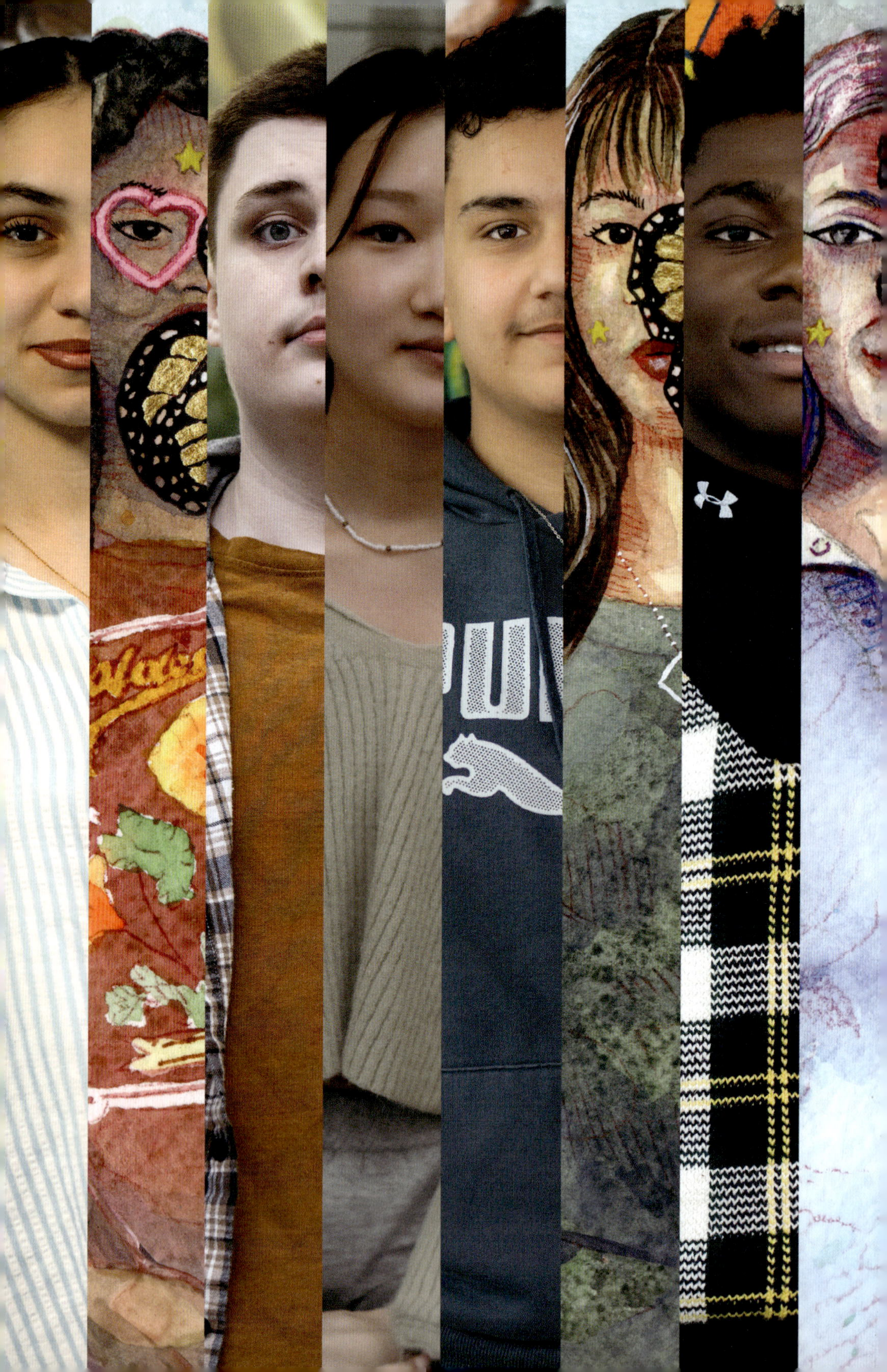

"These intimate stories from Chicago high school students arrive at a vital time when we need to be supportive of our immigrant and refugee neighbors. Through my work with refugees, I've seen how we can help build a spirit of welcoming when people learn about the trepidation, resilience, and hope that accompany so many newcomers' journeys. *Green Card Youth Voices: Immigration Stories from Chicago High Schools* is an exciting new opportunity to share voices that deserve to be heard."

—Melineh Kano, Executive Director, RefugeeOne

"*Green Card Youth Voices: Immigration Stories from Chicago High Schools* is a powerful collection that brings to life the personal journeys of young immigrants who now call Chicago home. Through their own words, these students share stories of resilience, determination, and courage—offering a window into the challenges and triumphs of building a new life in a new land. Their voices remind us of the strength found in diversity and the importance of listening with empathy. By sharing their experiences, these young authors help us grow as a community that welcomes, supports, and celebrates immigrants and refugees."

—Susan Sperry, Executive Director, World Relief Chicagoland

"Storytelling is a longstanding tradition in Arab culture, to pass along our history and share wisdoms. These stories do exactly that by voicing the challenges, strength, and joy of youth who have made the US their new home. There is wisdom throughout this book for everyone to learn from."

—Maya Atassi, Executive Director, Syrian Community Network, Chicago

"These stories shine with courage, vulnerability, and the unshakable strength of young people finding their voice. Each narrative in this collection is a radiant act of self-definition and a powerful reminder of how immigrant youth shape and enrich the soul of our city."

— Toufic El Rassi, Educator, Writer, and Artist

"As the granddaughter of an Italian immigrant to Chicago in the 1920s, I was privileged to read the powerful stories of these amazing young people. As I saw my grandmother's stories reflected in this current generation of young immigrants, I was moved to tears. Their incredible narratives tell the true story of what it is to be an American. The resilience, courage, humor and heartbreak of their stories allow us to remember the humanity behind the immigrant story. These are our children and the future of our country."

—Jennifer Ernsteen, Youth and Teen Program Coordinator, Vernon Area Public Library

"Thank you, Green Card Voices, for providing a space for us to hear from so many young people from around the world who have made their homes here in Chicago. In the years to come, migration will become more common than ever, and many more people will be displaced from their homes or seek safety from the climate emergency, wars, violence, and poverty. We all need stories such as these to prepare us for how we would like to meet the challenges ahead through our work as historians, educators, community members, and voters. This book is a revelation."

—Elena Gonzales, PhD, Curator of Civic Engagement and Social Justice,
Chicago History Museum

"*Green Card Voices Youth Voices: Immigration Stories from Chicago High Schools* is a meaningful writing project. Archiving these important personal narratives proves a useful gift for all readers who open this book and a testament to our shared humanity."

—Melissa Pavlik, Writing Center Director and Professor,
North Park University, Lewis University, and City Colleges of Chicago

"Not everyone has the courage and resilience these teens have to start over in a new country, to pursue their hopes and dreams, and to make their families proud. Stories like these should be required reading for all students as they learn about the world around them and how inspirational their neighbors are. Their persistence and perseverance will surely change the world one day."

—Rebecca Gibbons, Youth and Teen Librarian, Vernon Area Public Library

Green Card Youth Voices

Immigration Stories from Chicago High Schools

Christopher, Eva Yoo, Mussa Mrisho,
Anette Franco de la Torre, Gereltuya (Grace) Bayarmagnai,
Yelyzaveta (Lisa) Rozhkova, Yohana, Akili Dieudonne,
Yeseo (Esther) Jee, Fay, Bayarmagnai (Bay) Batochir,
Sebba Saad Allah, Douglas, Hamidah Binti Mohamad Ikbal,
Daeyun Lee, Tymur Tatsenyuk, Jhovanna, Nilarnab Roy,
Dariya Zhevakina, Joselyn, Aruuke Moldalieva,
Denis Dubovoi, Anastassiya Nartova, Josephine Akpai,
Alondra, Budgerel (Buka) Amarsanaa, Matviy Buyarskyy,
Andrea Verne, Nour Khashouk, Aranza

Authors

Julie Vang and Tea Rozman
Editors

ISBN: 978-1-949523-31-7
eISBN: 978-1-949523-32-4
LCCN: 2025912419

Printed in the United States of America
First Printing: 2025
20 19 18 17 16 5 4 3 2 1

Edited by Julie Vang and Tea Rozman

Cover and graphic design by Shiney Chi-Ia Her
Portrait illustrations by Pato Muñoz Vázquez
Photography and videography by Kou Lee

Green Card Voices
2611 1st Avenue South
Minneapolis, MN 55408
www.greencardvoices.org

Consortium Book Sales & Distribution
34 Thirteenth Avenue NE, Suite 101
Minneapolis, MN 55413-1007
www.cbsd.com

We dedicate this book to newcomers in Chicagoland and around the world.
May your journey be met with respect, your stories be heard,
and your dreams find a home.

Table of Contents

Foreword

The power of storytelling, for me, is about connection. I might have my own very personal experience—my life as an immigrant, as a man, as a husband—but when I tell my story, it creates a bridge. It allows other people to say, "*Yes, I've felt that too. I've been afraid too. I've had to start over too.*" That is the magic of stories. Even if our journeys are different, the emotions—loneliness, hope, sadness, determination—are the things that make us human. And that is how we begin to understand each other.

I came to this country when I was around fifteen years old, undocumented, and had a stutter. I did not speak English. I did not have a voice. I had to teach myself how to communicate, how to navigate a world where I felt as if I did not belong, not just through language, but through life. I stuttered, I stumbled, and like many of the young people in this book, I faced challenges I could not have imagined. But I kept going. I did not go to therapy because, like many who come from Latino families, I was taught that therapy was for crazy people or for the rich. I had to work through my struggles on my own. And eventually, I found my voice through storytelling.

It was not until I was about forty that I decided to confront my fear of public speaking. I had spent my whole life running from it. But one day, I put my name in a hat at a storytelling event—and with my wife's encouragement, I got up and told a story. I thought it was going to be a one-time thing. But that night, I won the competition. I went home and wrote five more stories that same night, and I realized: *This is what I was meant to do.*

Now, more than a decade later, I've had the honor of hearing stories from hundreds of immigrants and refugees, including the powerful voices in this book. What they're doing here isn't just writing. It's resisting. It's reclaiming. These students have lived through the unimaginable and are still willing to open their hearts to say, *This is who I am. This is what I carry.*

I see the same fire in the students in this anthology. In their words, I see strength. I see resilience. I see something that is too often overlooked in immigrant narratives: bravery in the face of the unknown, and a deep desire not just to survive, but to thrive—and to help others along the way. They didn't grow up saying, "*When I grow up, I want to be an immigrant or refugee.*" None of these kids planned to leave their home countries, their languages, or their families. They were forced by circumstance—by violence, by poverty, by politics—to make an unimaginable choice. And yet, here they are, learning a new language, navigating a new culture, starting from zero at the exact time in their lives when they are just supposed to be starting out. That takes a kind of courage that cannot be taught.

And they do so at a time when being an immigrant in America is not just difficult, it's dangerous. The political climate has made it clear: our presence is politicized, our families are criminalized, and even our citizenship can be questioned. We've seen green card holders deported, naturalized citizens detained, and people denied basic rights because of where they were born or what language they speak. It's cruel. It's unjust. And it's personal. Because I was once one of those kids, too. I still carry that fear.

Some say people like me should be quiet, grateful, and invisible. But I didn't survive all this just to be silent. I found my voice the hard way. And now I use it for the undocumented, for the queer and trans kids, for Black and Brown communities, for anyone who has ever been told they don't belong. I use it so others might feel less alone. That's what these stories do, too.

I was especially moved by Grace's story, and how she found her way back to music in the middle of her adjustment to American life—her violin, once a piece of her past in Mongolia, became a bridge to her new world and a reminder of everything she had already overcome. Matviy's story stayed with me too—how he carried the quiet beauty of his village in Ukraine and the trauma of war all the way to Chicago, now determined to help others going through similar paths. Then there is Fay, whose journey from Nigeria to Chicago is filled with so much movement and loss—yet she stands grounded, building vibrant school communities, embracing both her Nigerian identity and the layered reality of being Black in America with a wisdom far beyond her years. And Alondra, who speaks honestly about the uncertainty of her future as an immigrant, dreams of becoming a pilot or doctor even as she worries about whether she'll be allowed to stay, holding onto her hope and her love for her family like a compass guiding her forward.

These young people, these students, are not just telling their stories—they are planting seeds. I have seen it in workshops I have led, like the one at Truman College. I watched students walk in unsure of what they could say, unsure if their stories mattered—and five weeks later, they were standing on stage, walking, talking, making people laugh and cry. And I looked at them and thought, *You have no idea how powerful you are. But I see it. It's already blooming.*

One story that stayed with me is Christopher's. He and his family walked across multiple countries from Venezuela, through jungles and dangerous paths. And when they reached other countries, instead of help, they faced cruelty. People stole from them. They suffered. And yet, when Christopher tells his story, there is no anger. He talks about wanting to help others so that they do not have to go through what he did. That is the kind of strength that humbles you. That is the kind of heart that changes the world.

There is a saying I love: "*Being angry at someone is like drinking poison and hoping the other person will die.*" It took me a long time to understand that. But these kids? They already get it. They already know that healing and hope are stronger than hate.

So, to you—the reader—please listen. These stories are more than just words. They are lived experiences. They are acts of courage. Do not read them with pity. Read them with pride. Read them with love. See yourself in them, because these young people are your classmates, your neighbors, your future coworkers—and maybe even your future heroes.

— Nestor "the Boss" Gomez,
Former Undocumented Immigrant, Poet, Published Writer, Storyteller
Close-to-100-times Winner of the Moth StorySLAM
Creator of Immigration Storytelling Show *80 Minutes Around the World*

Acknowledgements

The creation of this nonfiction book was a trauma-informed, student-centered process intentionally designed to meet the unique needs of our young immigrant authors. Many of the students who shared their stories have experienced interrupted education and limited English proficiency, and they did so during a particularly challenging and politically charged time. Their courage and willingness to open up to us—and to the world—is what makes this book both powerful and necessary.

After the 2024 presidential election, new policies and political changes caused immediate uncertainty for many immigrants living in the United States with temporary legal status, who are still in the process of getting permanent residency. While these challenges became especially intense after 2024, many issues facing immigrants, such as systemic inequalities, anti-immigrant rhetoric, and government actions towards mass deportation, have existed under multiple administrations for many years. These ongoing challenges have often forced immigrants into silence, out of fear for their safety and future.

This book breaks that silence by sharing these first person stories of immigrants who are on the receiving end of this negative rhetoric in hopes of building empathy. Therefore, to protect the privacy of student authors and their families, some details have been altered. In certain cases, names of the authors and their family members have been changed or replaced with pseudonyms.

These students are also visually represented with mindful portrait illustrations by Pato Muñoz Vázquez. You will notice the faces in these illustrations are partially covered by a monarch butterfly. The monarch butterfly has become a symbol of immigration, representing the long journeys of immigrants finding a safe and welcoming home. Monarchs fly thousands of miles, adjusting their travel patterns as the world changes around them. Similarly, the student authors have travelled great distances to find peace and safety. The production of this book reflects the same care, with deliberate and respectful choices to honor each student author.

The heart and soul of this book are the thirty student authors, whose voices bring it to life. These young people—eleven boys and nineteen girls, all high school students—represent five continents: Asia, Europe, Africa, North America, and South America, and come from nineteen different countries. From classroom preparation and portrait sessions to video interviews and essay revisions, they demonstrated remarkable resilience, insight, and grace. We are immensely proud of each of them and deeply honored to share their stories, experiences, wisdom, and hope—so that we may all learn from *them*.

We would like to thank the three high schools represented in this project for their dedication, as well as our partner organization, the Chicago Refugee Coalition, for joining us in this important work.

This book would not have been possible without the unwavering commitment of twelve outstanding educators: Alma Tamayo, Justin Fisk, Kelley O'Reilly, Kamila Zaremba, Nicole Demarakis, Hanz Berduo, Delta Cervantes, Alondra Sepulveda, Mayra Ramirez, Rosemarie Markopoulos, Juliana Poshi, and Josh Zepeda. These devoted teachers did far more than guide—they nurtured, empowered, and stood beside each student author throughout the entire process. Their tireless efforts to identify and support student voices, coordinate with editors and the production team, and prepare each participant to share their story with confidence are the cornerstone of this work.

We're also grateful to our teacher liaison, Angelica Torralba Olague, who supported and created the training for educators to prepare the student authors for recording and sharing their stories.

To honor and uplift the voices of our student authors, we collaborated with filmmaker and photographer Kou Lee to create compelling video narratives, portraits, and the trailer. The videos were thoroughly reviewed by our senior video and media advisor, Michael Hay.

We are deeply grateful to our copyeditors, Gloria Narabrook and Susan Benson, who worked closely with students to revise each essay with care and attention. We also thank Abbie Phelps, who provided thoughtful edits to both the essays and the author biographies. Special thanks to Yixiu Chen, Adjunct Instructor for the Field Experience in the Leadership Minor at the University of Minnesota Twin Cities, for supporting this project by facilitating the placement of intern Riley Rasmussen, whose assistance with the essays and glossary was invaluable.

A heartfelt thanks to Shiney Chi-Ia Her, our graphic designer, who beautifully designed both the cover and the interior of this book. To Aaliyah Hannah, Co-Executive Director, as well as the Board of Directors of Green

Card Voices, thank you for your continued vision and support in bringing this project to life.

We are also deeply thankful to Connor M. Mautner, Founder & Strategic Director of the Chicago Refugee Coalition, who wrote the book's Introduction, and Nestor "the Boss" Gomez, who authored a thoughtful and powerful Foreword. Their contributions provided vital context and vision for the stories that follow.

We want to express our sincere thanks to Zaynab Abdi and Yanci Almonte Vargas, both of whom played a key role in the classroom as past authors and trainers. Zaynab generously shared her own experience as a *Green Card Youth Voices: Minneapolis* author and worked closely with the students to support their journey. She also led a public speaking training, equipping the young authors with the confidence to share their stories beyond the book.

Special thanks to our funder, Walder Foundation. Without your generous support, this publication would not have been possible.

And finally, on a personal note, we thank our partners, children, families, and friends for encouraging us to pursue our passion for storytelling and justice. Because of you—and the broader network of support we have received—Green Card Voices continues to fulfill its mission: to build bridges between immigrants and their communities by sharing first-person narratives that inspire empathy, understanding, and action.

We hope this book helps readers see immigrants and refugees not as statistics, but as individuals with rich lives, diverse talents, and powerful contributions to make.

With gratitude,
Julie Vang and Tea Rozman, Co-Editors; and Isabel Bethke, Editorial Advisor

Introduction

A Nation Built by Neighbors & Strangers

Human migration has shaped the land that would become the United States for millennia. Over 15,000 years ago, the ancestors of Native American peoples crossed Beringia, gradually settling across the continent and forming diverse civilizations throughout the western hemisphere.[1] When Europeans arrived in the late 15th century, they ushered in a new wave of migration, characterized by conquest, imperialism, and displacement. Colonies took root in these Indigenous lands and steadily displaced those who had long called this land home and reshaping it into what would become the United States.[2] Despite deep division and conflict, the idea of a nation of immigrants took hold, allowing this paradox to grow.

After the American Revolution (1775-1783), waves of immigrants arrived while facing resistance from those who had come before them. In the early 19th century, Germans and Irish fled their homelands due to economic hardship and political unrest. Many Irish took on hard labor in Northeastern cities, where they faced strong nativist hostility by the White Anglo-Saxon Protestants (WASPs)—a suspicion that remained pronounced throughout much of the 20th century.[3] Germans, often arriving with more resources, settled in farming communities across the Midwest. Some, like the Amish and Mennonites, preserved their faith, language, and traditions through a secluded and insular way of life. Today, traces of that heritage remain.

By the mid-19th century, debates over immigration were really about identity—who belonged and who didn't. Who was considered "American"? And who had the power to decide? These questions bubbled to the surface as waves of Chinese immigrants arrived on the West Coast. Many were seeking opportunity amid the California Gold Rush.[4] Their most iconic contribution was constructing the *Transcontinental Railroad*, a project that connected the Atlantic with the Pacific and forever

1. Hopkins, David M. "Cenozoic History of the Bering Land Bridge." Science 129, no. 3362 (1960): 1519-1528. https://www.science.org/doi/10.1126/science.129.3362.1519
2. Bolton, Herbert Eugene, and Thomas Maitland Marshall. *The Colonization of North America*, 1492-1783. Macmillan, 1920.
3. Moses, Paul. "When America Hated Catholics." *Politico Magazine*, September 13, 2015, https://www.politico.com/magazine/story/2015/09/anti-catholicism-in-america-213149/.
4. Ngai, Mae. "Chinese Gold Miners and the 'Chinese Question' in Nineteenth-Century California and Victoria," *Journal of American History* 101, no. 4 (2015): 1082–1105.

changed the heartland of the country.[5] Despite their contributions, Chinese immigrants faced intense hostility, fueled by racist stereotypes that cast them as "unassimilable." This led to the passage of the *Chinese Exclusion Act of 1882*—the first major federal law restricting immigration.[6] In cities like Chicago, persistent threats and racial tensions led the Chinese community south, ultimately leading to the establishment of Chinatown at Wentworth and Cermak in 1912.[7]

From Isolationism to Refuge: US Immigration Policy in the 20th Century

In early 20th-century America, isolation kept the US neutral in World War I until 1917, when President Wilson sought war after mounting German aggression. Though it raged for years, US intervention played a crucial role in securing an Allied victory.[8] Yet, the exclusionary impulse deepened in the 1920s, culminating in the *Immigration Act of 1924*, which drastically curtailed arrivals from Southern and Eastern Europe and outright banned immigration from Asia.[9] But the true cost of these policies became glaringly apparent in 1939. Just before the outbreak of World War II, the US turned away the *MS St. Louis*, a ship carrying over 900 Jewish refugees fleeing Nazi persecution.[10] Forced to return to Europe, more than a quarter of its passengers were later murdered in the Holocaust.[11] This tragedy underscored the consequences of restrictive immigration laws and foreshadowed a postwar shift in policy.

In the aftermath of World War II, the global political system underwent a dramatic realignment, with the US playing a leading role in shaping new international institutions such as the UN, IMF, and NATO.[12] The US facilitated the spread of liberal democratic norms in Western Europe and Japan while emerging as the dominant global power. However, the Soviet Union opposed this liberal order, leading to ideological and geopolitical divisions that shaped the Cold War and set the stage for future refugee outflows at the

5. White, Richard *Railroaded: The Transcontinentals and the Making of Modern America*. New York: Norton, 2011.
6. Kil, Sang Hea. "Fearing Yellow, Imagining White: Media Analysis of the Chinese Exclusion Act of 1882." *Social Identities* 18, no. 6 (2012): 663–77. https://doi.org/10.1080/13504630.2012.708995.
7. Ho, Chuimei, and Soo Lon Moy. *Chinese in Chicago, 1870-1945*. Arcadia Publishing, 2005.
8. Klein, Stefan. *America First? Isolationism in US Foreign Policy from the 19th to the 21st Century*. Master's thesis, Naval Postgraduate School, 2017.
9. Brinkmann, Tobias. "Review of *Who Gets In: An Immigration Story*, by Norman Ravvin." *Canadian Jewish Studies Études Juives Canadiennes*, 38 (Aug. 2024): 241-3, https://doi:10.25071/1916-0925.40387.
10. Ogilvie, Sarah A., and Scott Miller. *Refuge Denied: The St. Louis Passengers and the Holocaust.* (Madison: University of Wisconsin Press, 2010).
11. *Ibid.*
12. Grigorescu, Alexandru. *The Ebb and Flow of Global Governance: Intergovernmentalism versus Nongovernmentalism in World Politics.* (Cambridge: Cambridge University Press, 2020).

tail-end of the 20th century.[13]

This new global system ushered in a new era of American immigration policy. *The Displaced Persons Act* of 1948 provided refuge for those left stateless by war.[14] In 1951, the United Nations adopted the Refugee Convention, establishing the modern legal framework for refugee protection. Though the US did not sign the 1951 UN Refugee Convention, it joined the 1967 Protocol, which expanded refugee protections worldwide.[15]

By 1965, Congress passed the *Immigration and Nationality Act*, which marked a fundamental break from the restrictive quotas of the early 20th century, opening the doors to immigrants from Latin America, Asia, and Africa.[16] A decade later, *The Indochina Migration and Refugee Assistance Act of 1975* provided a pathway for approximately 130,000 Vietnamese, Cambodian, and Laotian refugees to resettle in the United States following the *Fall of Saigon*.[17]

More recent decades have seen migration patterns continue to shift, with waves of newcomers driven by economic opportunity, political instability, and climate displacement.[18] Each era of migration has reshaped the nation's social fabric, its cities, and its conflicts—and I submit that this is most visible in Chicago.

---

13. Mohamed S. Helal, "The Crisis of World Order and the Constitutive Regime of the International System," Florida State University Law Review 46 (2022): 345. https://ir.law.fsu.edu/lr/vol46/iss3/3; Loftus, Suzanne. *Russia, China And The West In The Post-Cold War Era: The Limits Of Liberal Universalism*. Palgrave Macmillan, 2024.
14. Hasson, Russel. *The Displaced Persons Act of 1948*. 1950. Bowling Green State University, Master's thesis. OhioLINK Electronic Theses and Dissertations Center, http://rave.ohiolink.edu/etdc/view?acc_num=bgsu1670316747948432.
15. McAdam, Jane, and G. Gilbert. "Special Issues to Commemorate the 70th Anniversary of the 1951 Convention Relating to the Status of Refugees." International Journal of Refugee Law 33, no. 2 (2021); Lin, C. *Examining Refugee Protection in Non-Signatories to the Refugee Convention and Protocol: Lessons Learned for the Taiwan* Context. OAPEN, 2024.
16. Hoffnung-Garskof, Jesse. "The Immigration Reform Act of 1965," in The Familiar Made Strange: American Icons and Artifacts after the Transnational Turn (Ithaca: Cornell University Press, 2015), https://www.degruyter.com/document/doi/10.7591/9780801455469-012/pdf?licenseType=restricted; Massey, Douglas S. and Pren, Karen A. "Unintended Consequences of US Immigration Policy: Explaining the Post-1965 Surge from Latin America," Population and Development Review 38, no. 1 (2012): 1–29, https://pmc.ncbi.nlm.nih.gov/articles/PMC3407978/pdf/nihms389585.pdf, https://onlinelibrary.wiley.com/doi/abs/10.1111/j.1728-4457.2012.00470.x.
17. Gerald R. Ford Presidential Library. *Fourth Report to the Congress on the Indochina Refugee Assistance Program*, June 30, 1975.
18. Balsari, Satchit et al. "Climate Change, Migration, and Civil Strife." *Current environmental health reports* vol. 7, 4 (2020): 404-414. https://doi:10.1007/s40572-020-00291-4. (review of global migration trends driven by economic challenges, political instability, and environmental shocks); Almulhim, A.I., Alverio, G.N., Sharifi, A. et al. Climate-induced migration in the Global South: an in depth analysis. npj Clim. Action 3, 47 (2024). https://doi.org/10.1038/s44168-024-00133-1 (rising temperatures, floods, droughts, and sea-level rise displacing millions); and M. Cipollina, L. De Benedictis, and E. Scibè, "Climate Change, Inequality, and Human Migration," Journal of the European Economic Association 20, no. 3 (2021): 1145–78.

The City of Strong Shoulders & Open Doors:

Chicago's history, like that of the nation, is a story of migration. Long before it became the metropolis we know today, it was a strategic trading post, first established by Jean Baptiste Point du Sable: a Black fur trader of Haitian descent who was the first non-native person to permanently reside in the area.[19] Settling at the mouth of the Chicago River, du Sable built a successful trading hub, laying the foundation for a city that would be shaped and reshaped by waves of newcomers.

From its earliest days, Chicago grew against the backdrop of the larger migration patterns that defined America. As settlers moved westward in the early 19th century, the city rapidly expanded, drawing Irish, German, and Scandinavian immigrants who built its canals, roads, and railways, turning it into the beating heart of the Midwest (sorry, Ohio).[20] By the late 19th century, the city's industrial boom brought waves of newcomers—Poles, Italians, and Jews from Eastern and Southern Europe.[21] Alongside them were thousands of African Americans from the South, escaping Jim Crow oppression during the Great Migration (1915–1974) after the failure to implement many reforms promised during Reconstruction.[22]

Many Black arrivals found guidance and opportunity through the *Chicago Defender*, the nation's most influential Black newspaper. *The Defender* published job listings, housing advertisements, and editorials encouraging African Americans to leave the South for economic opportunity and dignity in Chicago.[23] Once in the city, Black migrants helped shape Bronzeville, which came to be known as Chicago's Black Metropolis. Bounded by 31st Street to the north, Lake Michigan and Hyde Park to the east, and 51st Street to the south, the neighborhood emerged as a center of Black culture, commerce, and civic life.

As noted by Chicago poet Gwendolyn Brooks in A Street in Bronzeville:

> *'If you wanted a poem, you had only to look out of a window. There was material always, walking or running, fighting or screaming or singing.'* [24]

19. Crew, Spencer. "The Great Migration and African American Urban Life," in Black Migration: The Journey to Urban America (Washington, D.C.: National Museum of American History, 1998).
20. Køhlert, Frederik Byrn. *Chicago: A Literary History*. (Cambridge: Cambridge University Press, 2021).
21. *Ibid.*
22. Rocksborough-Smith, Ian Maxwell. *Contentious Cosmopolitans: Black Public History and Civil Rights in Cold War Chicago, 1942-1972*. University of Toronto, 2014.
23. Schlabach, Elizabeth Schroeder. *Along the Streets of Bronzeville: Black Chicago's Literary Landscape*. (Urbana: University of Illinois Press, 2017).
24. Brooks, Gwendolyn. A Street in Bronzeville. Library of America/Library Classics of the United States, Inc, 2014.

Her words captured the everyday beauty and complexity of a neighborhood whose cultural legacy rivaled that of Harlem in New York City.[25] From its jazz clubs and literary circles to its network of Black-owned businesses, Bronzeville embodied both the hardship and hope of a newly arrived community determined to build a better future.

What united all of these newcomers—Irish, Germans, Italians, Jews, Poles, Asians, and Black migrants—was the opportunity for something more: better wages, better job advancement, better educational opportunities, stable communities to raise families, and much more. Many of these hopes were realized on the floor of Chicago's various mills, railroad yards, and packing houses, where a vast majority of immigrants and Black workers found employment.[26] Their labor fueled Chicago's rise as an industrial and cosmopolitan powerhouse: a distinction the city continues to hold today.

19th and 20th Century: Eastern European and Balkan Migration

By the late 1800s, waves of Polish immigrants were pouring into Chicago, drawn by the promise of work and a fresh start. They came in such numbers that the city soon housed one of the largest Polish communities outside of the country, estimated at over 400,000 by the mid-20th century, with Chicago earning the nickname *Little Warsaw*.[27] These newcomers built churches, printed Polish newspapers, and opened community halls. Even as future generations moved outward into the suburbs, neighborhoods like Avondale and Jackowo remained proud and deeply rooted symbols of Polish life in Chicago.

At the same time, Ukrainian immigrants found refuge in the area now known as Ukrainian Village. Many had fled the Russian Empire, and later the Soviet regime. Their community steadily grew, welcoming post–World War II refugees and, in more recent years, those escaping the violence of Russia's 2014 annexation of Crimea. Then came 2022, and another wave—this time, over 20,000 Ukrainians displaced by the full-scale invasion, according to US Customs and Border Protection. Through it all, Ukrainian Village has held strong, anchored by its Orthodox cathedrals, cultural centers, and a

25. Pacyga, Dominic A. *Slaughterhouse: Chicago's Union Stock Yard and the World It Made*. (Chicago: The University of Chicago Press, 2018), 2-4.
26. Abbott, A., Abbott, M., and Abbott, R. S. "Small Shops of the City: Growth of Chicago's Immigrant Neighborhoods." In Chicago: A Literary History, edited by Frederik Byrn Køhlert. Cambridge: Cambridge University Press, 2021.
27. Pacyga, Dominic A. *Chicago: A Biography*. (Chicago: University of Chicago Press, 2011).

deep sense of resilience passed from one generation to the next.[28]

In the 1990s, the wars that tore through the former Yugoslavia sent shockwaves across Europe—and thousands of refugees across the Atlantic. Many fled not just conflict, but the horrors of ethnic cleansing, mass displacement, and collapsed civil order.[29] Chicago became a sanctuary, and within it, Albany Park stood out as a haven. By the mid-1990s, it became home to a growing community of Bosnians, Serbs, Croats, and Kosovar Albanians seeking to rebuild lives fractured by war.[30] Today, the neighborhood bears witness to that layered inheritance: halal butchers beside taquerías, Bosnian spoken alongside Arabic, Spanish, and Korean.[31]

20th Century Growth: Latino Migration

By the early 20th century, Mexican immigrants began arriving in Chicago, filling labor shortages in the steel mills, railroad yards, and packing houses. While Mexican migration slowed during the Great Depression, it surged again in the mid-to-late 20th century due to economic instability and political unrest in Mexico. Many are now settled in Little Village (*La Villita*). For decades, and to this day, the community remains one of the largest Mexican-American neighborhoods in the US, known for its vibrant markets, festivals, and a strong sense of community continuously reinforced by new arrivals.

Alongside this growth, Chicago also became home to other Latino communities. Puerto Ricans arrived in large numbers after World War II, especially following their US citizenship in 1917, settling primarily in neighborhoods like Humboldt Park. More recently, Venezuelans and Colombians fleeing political crises and economic hardship have added to the new waves of migration.

21st Century: African and Middle Eastern Refugees in Rogers Park

The turn of the 21st century saw a significant rise in African migration to Chicago, driven by a series of devastating conflicts across the continent. The Somali Civil War, the Second Congo War, violence in Sudan and South Sudan, and Eritrea displaced millions. In recent years, refugees from Syria,

28. Yekelchyk, Serhy. *Ukraine: What Everyone Needs to Know*. Oxford University Press, 2020.
29. Wright, Ellen J. *Bosnians in Chicago: Transnational Activities and Obstacles to Transnationalism*. 2000.
30. Croegaert, Ana. *Bosnian Refugees in Chicago Gender, Performance, and Post-War Economies*. Lexington Books, 2020.
31. *Valenta, Marko, and Sabrina P. Ramet. The Bosnian Diaspora: Integration in Transnational Communities*. Routledge, 2016.

Palestine, and Afghanistan, driven by civil war, occupation, and political upheaval, have also found safety in the area. Together, these communities helped shape Rogers Park into one of Chicago's most diverse and resilient neighborhoods.

Late 20th and 21st Century: Immigrants in Greater Chicago

Buffalo Grove has become home to thriving Japanese, Indian, Korean, and a growing number of Russian, Uzbek, Kazakh, Kyrgyz, Ukrainian, and Mexican families. Drawn by top-rated schools, job opportunities, and a safe environment, families have established deep roots, contributing to civic life, religious centers, and local businesses. Over one-third of Buffalo Grove's population is now foreign-born.

In Vernon Hills, a wave of immigrants who are Indian, Chinese, Korean, and Filipino families make up a significant portion of the population, with newcomers from Uzbekistan, Kazakhstan, and Russia. Many arrived in the early 2000s for employment in tech, healthcare, and engineering fields. The suburb has since seen a rise in Asian grocery stores, restaurants, and community spaces that reflect this growing diversity.

Lincolnshire and Riverwoods, though smaller, mirror these trends with an influx of Indian, Mongolian, and Korean residents, along with Eastern European immigrants. These communities are often highly educated professionals who seek suburban quality of life while remaining connected to Chicago's economic centers via nearby transit routes.

This suburban shift represents more than just a change of address. Immigrant families in these areas are shaping school districts, participating in local governance, and redefining what cultural identity looks like in predominantly white, upper-middle-class suburbs. The presence of temples, mosques, language schools, and community festivals speaks to the rich cultural layers that immigrants are adding to the suburban Midwest.

We Hold These Truths: Stories Are Echoes of a Shared Reality

Chicago's story is one of legendary figures, monumental progress, and earth-shattering moments.[32]

32. Chicago's history is marked by pivotal events that have shaped both the city and the nation. What follows is a list of some of the most significant and defining events in the city's history; however, it is far from exhaustive: The Fort Dearborn Massacre (1812) underscored early settler-Native American conflicts, while the Great Chicago Fire (1871) spurred rapid reconstruction. The Haymarket Riots (1886) ignited the labor movement, and the Chicago Race Riots (1919) exposed deep racial tensions amid postwar migration. The Black Panther Party's Chicago chapter (1960s), led by Fred Hampton, became a force in civil rights before his assassination in a police raid. The Chicago School of Sociology redefined urban studies, and in a mo-

But just as a river carves through canyons, quieter voices have also shaped the city in equally important ways. The book you are holding is a collection of such accounts—chronicles told by softer voices, frequently from the margins of society, sharing the narratives that are too often overlooked but nonetheless impact our city, our neighborhoods, and our shared urban identity. Stories matter—if not to reach an audience, then to affirm ourselves. They are our lifeblood, grounding us in a sense of place and identity while shaping our understanding of the world. Stories create pathways to belonging, connecting us to a broader community. They are also vessels for history, with each retelling breathing new life into the past. Most importantly, stories honor those who came before us—the trailblazers who laid the foundations of where we stand today as we build our shared tomorrow.

Migration to Chicago has never followed a single path. Once, it was industrial work that drew people—mill jobs, stockyards, the promise of something steady. Today, the routes are less uniform: asylum claims, student visas, tech startups, and care work form the melange of new arrivals settling everyday. Refugees arrive alongside international scholars. Delivery drivers hold advanced degrees. What unites them isn't the paperwork but the quiet consideration of *what would be their best bet in this new land:* that this city might offer a foothold to build anew. That it might not only be a place to survive, but to thrive.

They don't just come for opportunity. They come because someone else did. A name in a group chat. A cousin already here. A neighborhood that *sounds* familiar even when nothing else does. The story of a life that made it—barely, maybe, but made it all the same.

Chicago's immigrant communities have always been built this way: through informal networks, borrowed apartments, faith communities, and the kind of ordinary repetition that slowly becomes a life.

A weekly grocery run.

A second shift.

A language class in a church basement.

---

ment of citywide unity, the Cubs' 2016 World Series victory ended a 108-year drought, cementing its place in sports history. Together, these events capture the city's defining rhythm: a pattern of rupture, resistance, and reinvention. See: Pacyga, Dominic A. *Chicago: A Biography* University of Chicago Press, 2009; Duis, Perry R. *Challenging Chicago: Coping with Everyday Life, 1837–1920.* University of Illinois Press, 1998.; Goldsby, Jacqueline. *A Spectacular Secret: Lynching in American Life and Literature.* University of Chicago Press, 2006; Haas, Jeffrey. *The Assassination of Fred Hampton: How the FBI and the Chicago Police Murdered a Black Panther.* Lawrence Hill Books, 2009.

In moments of upheaval, that's what people seek—not some grand reinvention, but continuity. Something that holds—quietly, steadily—so that hope can endure.

After all, where there is *hope*, there is life. And where there is *life*, there are *stories to be told.*

— Connor M. Mautner,
Founder & Strategic Director of the Chicago Refugee Coalition

How to Use this Book

At the end of each student's essay, you will find a URL link to that student's digital narrative on Green Card Voices' website. You will also see a QR code link to that story. Below are instructions for using your mobile device to scan a QR code.

1. Using your mobile device—such as a smartphone or tablet—visit the App Store for your network, such as the Apple Store or the Android Store. Search the App Store for a "QR reader." You will find multiple free apps for you to download, and any one of them will work with this book.

2. Open your new QR reader app. Once the app has opened, hover the camera on your mobile device a few inches away from the QR code you want to scan. The app will capture the image of the QR code and take you to that student's profile page on the Green Card Voices website.

3. Once your web browser opens, you'll see the digital story. Press play and watch one of our inspirational stories.

STEP 1

Open up your phone camera OR download the app.

Available on the App Store

Available on the Android App Store

STEP 2

Scan the QR code.

STEP 3

Watch the digital story.

Mexico
Panama
Venezuela
Colombia
Peru
Chile
Green Card Youth Voices storytellers' countries of origin
Green Card Youth Voices storytellers' countries of residence or nationality

World Map

Russia
Italy
Kazakhstan
Mongolia
Ukraine
Kyrgyzstan
Uzbekistan
South Korea
Lebanon
Syria
Jordan
Guam
Nigeria
India
Ghana
Tanzania
Malaysia

Personal Essays

SOUTH AMERICA
Venezuela

Christopher

Born: Venezuela

"THE REASON MY FAMILY LEFT TO GO TO THE US WAS THAT IT WAS THE ONLY COUNTRY THAT CAME IN TO HELP US, AND THE ONLY COUNTRY THAT HEARD THE STORY OF WHAT OUR PEOPLE WERE GOING THROUGH."

I was born in Venezuela. I am fifteen years old. I have a little sister. I lived in a coastal city. In the summer, we go to the beach, play with the sand, build castles, or do things like that. With my family, we play soccer or volleyball.

In my home in Venezuela, I lived with my grandmother and my sister because my mom was not there at the time. One day, my mom made a video call to me. She told me she wanted me and my sister to leave Venezuela because the economy and security were not good. She did not like that and looked for a better life for my sister and me. She made the decision to go to the United States for a better life for our family. We left everything—my family, my cousins, my uncles, my friends, my soccer team, and my pets. We left everything to come to the United States.

I started in my coastal town. We traveled through seven countries. We stayed in the first country for one week or more. In the next stop, there was a jungle. We stayed inside the jungle for three days or more. We did not have food, clothes, or shoes—nothing. My uncle suffers from diabetes. He cannot walk much. He cannot eat any food, so he needs specific food. Later in the second day, at night, he was just lying on the ground. He could not walk. He could not talk. He could not eat. Nothing. We stayed with him for like three hours. At night, like 10:00 p.m., we finished our travel through the jungle and entered into a refugee center, but after a while we could not stay there anymore.

We stayed at the next stop in a hotel for like three days. At our next stop, we traveled on the bus all day. We could not stay there long because it was too hard. At night, we walked for four hours with more people because it was so dangerous. At 2:00 a.m., we finished walking and stayed in the next country.

We stayed there for one or two weeks because we needed a permit to walk freely. In the second to last stop it was hard. Most people were stealing from the other people. One day, we were waiting for the bus to the next country. That day, we did not have food, we did not have money, and I had a phone. I was going to sell it to another person for money. But that person—I do not know who—they stole my phone, so we did not have money. We did not have food, nothing to eat.

The next day, we took a bus to the next country. It was so hard for me because of the security. They were stealing money, and we did not have money. The police told us to get off the bus and go back to where we started; we walked from there. We walked for hours. It was so hard for my family. After that, we finally made it to the last country, the United States.

First, we arrived in Texas together. My uncle and cousin left first for Chicago. An immigrant shelter in Texas helped me and my family with money to go to Miami, where we stayed for a month. Later, my mom got money and decided to go to Chicago with me and my sister to be with my uncle and my cousin so the family could be together.

The first day in the US was so hard because the people talked in other languages and we did not understand. We did not have money, we did not have food, we did not have a home to sleep in or things like that. It was so hard. We stayed in Texas for a week. That week was so hard for my family. I did not like it. The immigrant shelter helped me and my family with food, clothes, and money. The immigrant shelter paid for our bus tickets to go to Miami. I studied for one month, and after that, we went to Chicago.

I arrived in Chicago in December 2023. The first day and week, it was so hard, because we did not know anyone. There were like 500 people in the immigrant shelter. We did not know who those people were, and it was hard for all of us. The food was not good. Two months later, the immigrant shelter in Chicago helped me and my sister start school. That was great.

Now, my life is very good here in Chicago, because I have my family. I started school. I have good grades and good attendance. My mom works so hard every day for our family. I like that. My life now is perfect.

I want to study computer engineering. I want to help the immigrants with money and things like that. I want to be kind to immigrants. I want to help them. People insulted me, and they did not see me in a good way, so they did not help me. Do not blame me. We did not understand the language at the time. We did not understand what was happening. We did not know. My mom did not speak English, so it was hard for her. My little sister too. But now, since staying here in Chicago, my English is better, so I have the opportunity for a better life. I can talk with Americans, and I can help my mom translate and things like that.

VIDEO LINKS

greencardvoices.org/speakers/christopher

AUSTRALIA & OCEANIA
Tamuning,
Guam

Eva Yoo

Born: Tamuning, Guam **Raised:** Seoul, South Korea

"IN KOREA, MOST PEOPLE ARE KOREAN, BUT HERE, I MET FRIENDS FROM MANY DIFFERENT COUNTRIES, WHICH WAS NEW AND EXCITING FOR ME."

I was born in Guam because of my father's job there. My family lived there when both my sister and I were born, and we stayed until 2009. After that, we moved to Seoul, the capital of Korea. I do not have as many memories of Guam as my parents and sister do because I was too young. However, I do remember going back during the holidays; those visits were always fun because we had many friends there. I loved swimming in the ocean and enjoying the beautiful surroundings. I really enjoyed the pristine nature of Guam. I missed that while living in Seoul, which is a large city with ten million people—very urban, with busy traffic and barely any nature.

Growing up in Korea, my childhood was simple. For a long time, I even thought I was born there until my mom told me otherwise. It was a shock to realize that I was not actually born there. I was about ten years old when I learned that I was born in Guam, which is an organized, unincorporated territory of the United States in Micronesia (a subregion of the western Pacific Ocean). Because of that, I have been a US citizen since birth.

In my family, I have one older sister who currently goes to the same school as me here in the US. She is a senior. Back in Korea, we used to fight every day, like most siblings do—and frankly, that has not changed after the move. As for my hobbies, I have always loved art, in particular oil painting on canvas. My parents have always supported us in our artistic interests by buying us art supplies and signing us up for art classes.

The decision to move to the US happened unexpectedly. One day, when I was in seventh grade, my dad called me and my sister and gave us two options: We could either move to another city within Korea—an academically competitive city—or move to America to continue our high school education. I would not have had much confidence in my academic success had I stayed in Korea because it is so competitive. For that reason, I chose to move to the US to finish my high school.

My parents chose Chicago, though I do not know exactly why. Maybe it was because of the school, which is diverse and highly regarded. However, I do not live with my parents right now—I stay with a host family. My sister and I came here alone, without our parents, which was a huge sacrifice, but at least we have each other. I can only see my parents once a year, and being away from them has been really hard. I also had to leave behind my friends in Korea, which was another major challenge.

My first experience in the US was really difficult. I have high anxiety, and without my parents or familiar support, I felt very unstable. The language barrier was one of the biggest challenges. I was not good at speaking English, and I often could not understand what people were saying to me. However, once I was in the US, my seventh-grade teacher, who was Korean, helped me adjust and become more comfortable. I am really grateful to her.

There were also cultural differences that surprised me. For example, in Korea, students stay in the same classroom all day while teachers come to them for different subjects. Here, I had to move to a new classroom for every period, which was shocking at first. Another difference was diversity. In Korea, most people are Korean, but here, I met friends from many different countries, which was new and exciting for me.

Now, my life in the US feels much more stable compared to when I first arrived. I have made great friends from different backgrounds, and I really love that. Also, in Korea I was not the type to hang out with friends often—I preferred staying home, listening to music, and relaxing on weekends. That part of me has not changed much, but I do appreciate the friendships I have built here.

Looking ahead, I hope to give back to my community by helping other transfer students like me. My middle school teacher helped me so much, and I want to do the same for others. I would love to help translate for students who struggle with English to make their transition easier. I also really appreciate my host family for providing us with a home, food, and support. They even help with transportation, since I cannot drive yet.

The kindness of all the people I have met here— whether my host family, my teachers, or friends—has made a huge difference in my journey, and I am grateful for everything they have done.

VIDEO LINKS

greencardvoices.org/speakers/eva-yoo

DRAKE
UNIVERSITY
AFRICA
Kigoma,
Tanzania

Mussa Mrisho

Born: Kigoma, Tanzania

"THE REASON MY FAMILY LEFT TO GO TO THE US WAS THAT IT WAS THE ONLY COUNTRY THAT CAME IN TO HELP US, AND THE ONLY COUNTRY THAT HEARD THE STORY OF WHAT OUR PEOPLE WERE GOING THROUGH."

I was born in Kigoma, Nyarugusu, a refugee camp in Tanzania. My parents flew to Tanzania because there was a war in Congo. Many people were dying, and it was very hard for them to survive there. Although I was not born yet, my parents had to wait about twenty years to get to come to the USA. I only lived in Tanzania for seven years, and then I came here.

Growing up in the refugee camp, life was decent, but it could have been better. I grew up with my grandparents, since my mother had me at fifteen years old, and my dad was seventeen years old. They were still developing since they were still kids. Both my parents had to go to school.

My grandparents took me to the store. I got everything that I needed, like clothes, school supplies, and other stuff. I had multiple friends. All the houses were mostly made out of mud. The bathroom was a very deep hole that the people volunteered to dig together. It was very deep to make sure that the smell does not come to the surface.

Education was decent, but it could have been much better. I felt that most of the teachers were very strict for no reason, and the punishments were very cruel. I grew up playing soccer with my cousins and friends, and the ball that we played with was a little ball made out of air, wrapped around in multiple bags over and over until it had a little weight on it. Therefore, you could kick it and it would not float into the air.

I also helped my grandparents. My grandmother had a farm. After school or on days that I did not go to school, I took some of the animals and went to feed them. Since there was not much grass in the area, it was mostly mud. You had to walk a couple of miles or more to even see grass.

Getting water was pretty difficult, since there was only one well in the area. It was not near the village, and people had to walk most of the time. It was not the boys who were walking to get there to get water; it was mostly girls, and they walked more than a mile to get there and then come back. When they were there, they had to wait in a big line, since multiple people were trying to get water just to cook food, or even just to make sure that their plates were clean.

Some of the traditional food that we ate was fufu. Usually, my parents made fufu with corn flour and boiling water. With fufu, you wait and stir it around until it becomes solid, so that you can pick it up with your hands. On the side, you can have any sort of soup. A soup could be chicken soup, vegetable soup, anything. Another thing that we ate most of the time was rice and beans. This was usually what we ate, since it was cheap and what our family could afford.

When I was informed that I would be moving to the United States, my family told me that it would only be me and my mother moving, not my grandpa, not my grandma, not my cousins, not my dad. We were a big family, and the idea of leaving them and just being me and my mom was very depressing. I did not even want to move and leave them alone, even though it was a better chance for me to live a better life and get better stuff, because they are my everything. They are my life. They are the reason I live, and without them, I do not know how I would be in the world.

The reason my family left to go to the US was that it was the only country that came in to help us, and the only country that heard the story of what our people were going through. They decided to volunteer and help us come for a better life. So my family and I decided to move to the US to look for better opportunities and a better life.

In Tanzania, resources and education were very limited, especially for young people. For example, even if someone had a master's degree or any kind of education, finding a job was still really hard for many parents. It was very hard for families to figure out what their kids were going to have to eat and what kind of meal they were going to have the next day, or even the next week. Families would go days, sometimes even weeks, without food. It was a constant struggle we were living through. The government did not provide any resource of help or assistance to its people, so people were only relying on themselves and what their families could do.

The journey basically started when we were informed that we were going to be leaving Tanzania. But before we actually went to America, we first had to go to this other place. We traveled to a different city, and stayed in a big building with all the other people who were also going to America with us, all flying on the same plane. We stayed there for a couple of months. The place actually gave us food, shelter, and everything we needed. Most of the things we needed to prepare for America, like coats and shoes, were all provided for us before we left.

Before getting on the real big plane to America, we first got on a very small plane. It felt like there were only about thirty to fifty people on it. It was just my mom and me going to the US, but on the plane, there were other people we knew from Nyarugusu who were also traveling to America.

When we first arrived, we did not just go straight to Chicago. First, we went to different countries. I think we went to Dubai first, then to the United Kingdom, and then finally to America. Everyone was being placed in different locations. Not everyone was going to the same place.

When my mom and I came to the US in 2016, we already had some family who had arrived earlier. They had been in America for a couple of years already. So, when we first came, we stayed with them before we got our own place.

Leaving behind some of my family, who stayed back in Africa so that my mom and I could have more opportunities, was really hard. Later, my grandparents and my grandma came, but it took a long time. I did not see my dad for most of my life. He recently just came around 2022. That was the first time I had seen him in many years. My grandparents came about five years after I did.

My first day in Chicago was actually kind of funny. In Africa, we were always told that America was very cold, that it was only cold all the time. So even on the plane, I was wearing this big jacket that came down to my knees. But when we arrived, it was summer. It was so hot. People were looking at us funny because we were the only ones wearing huge jackets. Then we got into an Uber. We drove past downtown, and when I saw the buildings, it was amazing. I saw lights, big buildings, tall buildings, small buildings. I saw so many people walking along the sidewalks. It was amazing to see things I had never seen in my life before. I never knew lights could be so bright. I never knew buildings could be that tall. I had never seen a glass building before. I just kept thinking, How did they even build this? How is this possible?

It was also my first time being in a small car. I had been in buses before, but never in a small car. It was a great experience. When the car was driving, it felt like it was going so fast. I even almost threw up inside the car. It was kind of funny, but it was also a great experience.

When school started in the fall, I noticed that the weather had suddenly changed from sunny most of the time to windy and cold, and snow started falling, which was something I was not used to. Adapting to the new weather was very difficult, but now I am used to it.

School in America was great. The education was great, and the teachers were really amazing. On my first day of school, even though I did not know the language, which was a big challenge, a teacher came to me with a computer. She used Google Translate to help me with everything I needed. If we were doing math, she would translate it for me. If we were doing English work, she would help me by translating it into Swahili so that I could understand. That was such a great opportunity for me. I also saw that here, kids were given so many chances to become whatever they wanted to become. They had multiple opportunities to earn what they wanted in life.

One of the biggest challenges for me at first was learning the language. But with the help of multiple teachers and the support from school, I was able to learn English quickly. Another opportunity I had here was being able to play soccer with an actual ball and on a real team. Our school had a soccer team. When the teacher asked me what sport I liked, I said soccer, and he told me to join the soccer team.

In Tanzania, schools did not have teams like that. We would just go outside with friends and play for fun. You never thought about becoming a professional soccer player or anything like that. But through school here, my teacher and later my coach saw that I was decent at soccer, and they signed me up for a real club team, Chicago City. I still play for them today. I am very grateful for the opportunity because it allowed me to expand my skills and my soccer abilities, and to dream about hopefully reaching a higher level one day.

Right now, my life is a little more complicated. I am a junior in high school. I have to do a lot of things like internships, studying, and soccer. My daily schedule is basically: wake up, go to school, come home, do homework, go to soccer practice, come back home, do some more studying. Most of the time, I am not really home that much. I mean, I get to see my family, but not as much as I want to.

I am currently part of two different programs. One of them is called the Fellowship Initiative. It is a program that helps youth like me explore different colleges and opportunities. For example, during spring break, while many students stayed home or traveled with their families, I had to go on a college tour with other students, visiting different colleges that I could apply to in the future. Although it was a great experience, I would have loved to spend that time with my family, because my schedule does not really give me much time to be with them.

For my future, in the next five to ten years, I first plan to go to college and get my major in accounting. I love math. I have always loved math, even when I was back in Africa. Math was one of those skills that, when I came to the US, I picked up quickly. I have always had a passion for it. I also want to keep playing soccer in college. Soccer is one of my passions. I am still playing right now, and I am working to expand my skills, so that maybe I can have a chance to play soccer in college.

After college, I plan to get a job as an accountant, because I love accounting. I feel like being an accountant will give me the opportunity to provide for my family, my mom, my cousins, and everyone who helped me. I also want to be able to give back to all the people who supported me in my life, to go back to them in the future and give them whatever they need, or any support they might need from me.

VIDEO LINKS

greencardvoices.org/speakers/mussa-mrisho

SOUTH AMERICA
Tepatitlán de Morelos, Jalisco, Mexico

Anette Franco de la Torre

Born: Tepatitlán de Morelos, Jalisco, Mexico

"WHEN I STARTED PACKING, IT HIT ME: HOW DO YOU PACK AN ENTIRE LIFE INTO TWO SUITCASES?"

I was born in Mexico—specifically in Tepatitlán de Morelos, Jalisco, a small city about an hour from Guadalajara. When I went to high school, I was excited because it was right after the pandemic—I finally had the chance to go back to school, and high school had been my dream since I was a kid. On the first day of school, I was nervous because I wondered if I would make friends. Still, I was happy to be there. At that time, I felt a sense of freedom, as if my life were just beginning. Before that, I often felt like I was stuck, like I was not really living. High school changed that for me—it was a place where I had responsibilities, but also could grow independently.

That April was particularly exciting because, in my city, we celebrate what we call "Tepabril," a month-long fair. Each city in Jalisco has its own celebration, but ours lasts the whole month. The fair includes concerts, exhibitions, and competitions like "Expo Ganadera," where animals are presented and judged. Every night, the town square comes alive with music and vendors; around 10:00 or 11:00 p.m., we have a "Castillo," a tower of fireworks that creates a beautiful show. That year was the first time I experienced the fair with my friends instead of just my family. I was thrilled, but also sad because I knew it would be my last one. Since the fair is not in the summer, I realized that returning to Mexico for it would be unlikely.

High school in Mexico is divided into semesters, meaning I only completed one four-month semester before leaving. During that time, I made friends and felt like they would be my friends for life. My family also had traditions, especially during "Semana Santa" (Holy Week, or Easter). Every year, we went to my grandparents' "rancho"—not quite a farm, but a rural place where we camped with the whole family for the weekend. We played, had bonfires, roasted marshmallows, and engaged in religious traditions. It was always a fun and special time.

My whole family is in Mexico, except for a few aunts who live in the US.

My mother's side is in San Miguel el Alto, while my father's side is in Tepatitlán. Family is very important in Mexico, and we always stayed close. Every fifteen days, we visited my grandparents at the rancho, bringing food to share. It was always a big gathering. Sometimes, it was boring when my cousins were not there, but I enjoyed watching the older relatives play cards and bet pesos. I played with them sometimes, though I usually lost all my money because they were so good at the game. My life in Mexico was wonderful.

I always knew that moving to the US was a possibility because my grandfather had a green card, and my dad applied through him. However, I never took it seriously. One day when I was ten, the day before Christmas—what we call "Noche Buena"—my dad told me that we might get a call in January. If that happened, we would move to the US in April. I did not quite understand what he meant, but I was excited. At ten years old, I was not thinking about the future. I was just excited about all the toys I saw on YouTube that I could not get in Mexico. But they never called, so I forgot about it.

Years later, in September 2021, my dad came home and said, "They called. We need to fly to Ciudad Juárez in less than a month to complete the paperwork for our green cards." I was in shock—everything was happening so fast. We had to buy plane tickets, book hotels, and schedule appointments, all of which were very expensive. When we arrived in Ciudad Juárez, the process involved a lot of paperwork, medical exams, and vaccines, which hurt a lot. I kept asking my dad, "What if they don't approve us?" But he reassured me, saying, "They have no reason to deny us. Don't worry."

Eventually, our green cards were approved, and my dad told me, "We're moving in June." That was only a few months away. I was in high school and did not want to leave. At first, we had to decide where to live—Palm Springs or Chicago—since we had family in both places. I chose Chicago because I wanted to see snow, and I hated hot weather.

My dad moved first, in January, to find a job and an apartment so that when my mom, my sister, and I arrived, we would be more comfortable. But it was not easy. Every landlord told him, "You don't have credit, so you can't rent an apartment." I did not understand why credit was so important here. By June, we still had not found a place, and we did not even have plane tickets because they were so expensive. I was secretly happy about that because I did not want to leave.

Finally, a landlord agreed to rent to us if we paid three months of rent up front. Once we had an apartment, my dad started buying the essentials—

beds, a fridge, food—and sending us pictures, asking for our opinions. I was still in denial about the move, but when I started packing, it hit me: how do you pack an entire life into two suitcases? I listened to music to distract myself, but when a song about leaving home played, I broke down crying. I had felt like my life was finally beginning—I had real friends and a relationship, I could make my own decisions, I could hang out, I was in high school. Suddenly, I had to leave everything behind.

On July 6, 2022, the day of our flight, my friends came over early in the morning to say goodbye. They brought gifts—one gave me a framed photo of all of us, and my boyfriend gave me a necklace shaped like half a heart, saying, "This is part of my heart. You'll take it with you to the US." It was an emotional day, but I had no choice. The moment had arrived.

We flew into Chicago at 3:00 a.m. My dad picked us up. We went to hug him after five long months without seeing him. He took us to a grocery store that was open twenty-four hours. My sister and I were fascinated—there were over 100 different kinds of cereal! We played with the shopping carts and asked my dad, "Can we buy this? Can we buy that?"

When we got to our apartment, I saw my new home for the first time. My dad had sent pictures, but it was different seeing it in person. My room only had a mattress because he had not assembled the bed yet. The first thing I did was unpack the framed photo from my friends and place it beside my bed. Then, exhausted, we all fell asleep.

Over the next few weeks, we focused on setting up our home, buying furniture, and getting used to shopping in dollars instead of pesos. Then, two weeks later, school started.

My sister and I went to school early; a Latina transfer buddy walked us to class. I first went to English class and realized I was in the wrong class—it was intermediate, but I was supposed to be in the beginning English class. I was nervous because I was the only student who spoke Spanish. Then one of the teachers came over and spoke Spanish to me. I felt more comfortable because they had noticed I did not want to talk at all. My classmates were so nice—they invited me to eat with them. Being alone at lunch was my biggest fear, and now I had them to sit with.

The bus was stressful. My sister and I walked all over the parking lot looking for the bus and finally found it. The next problem was that we did not know our bus stop back home. We only remembered my dad told us to get out of the first stop. Then we saw our parents were at the corner waiting for us so we would not get lost.

The second day of school, I went to my actual English class. The teacher gave us candy, and I realized everyone else in the class was like me and did not know English. I was more confident since I got candy and everyone was so nice. I did not feel ashamed. My classmates were my first friends and became my family at school.

Adjusting to school was overwhelming. Everything was different—the language, the way classes were structured, even how students paid for lunch. I was nervous every day, but little by little, I adapted.

Now, my life is busy. I come home at 7:00 p.m. on weekdays because I have fencing practice after school. On Saturdays, I go to ice skating classes. I love trying new things because I did not always have those opportunities in Mexico. My hobbies now include reading, fencing, ice skating, and playing guitar.

One of the things I love doing is helping new Latino students who arrive at my school. I introduce myself, ask about their schedules, and let them know they are not alone. I want them to feel comfortable, to know that even though moving to a new country is hard, they will be okay. Maybe, by sharing my story, others will find something to relate to and feel less alone.

A book lasts forever. I hope my story helps someone, even years from now, to know that they are not alone in this journey.

VIDEO LINKS

greencardvoices.org/speakers/anette-franco-de-la-torre

ASIA
Ulaanbaatar,
Mongolia

Gereltuya (Grace) Bayarmagnai

Born: Ulaanbaatar, Mongolia

"WHEN I WAS YOUNG, MY MOM ENROLLED ME IN VARIOUS CLUBS, SUCH AS MONGOLIAN DANCE AND SINGING. I ALSO PLAYED THE PIANO AND THE VIOLIN."

My name is Grace, and I was born in Ulaanbaatar, the capital of Mongolia. I am the youngest child in my family. My mother and older sister were also born in Ulaanbaatar, while my father is from another region of Mongolia. I lived in Mongolia until I was fourteen, before moving to the United States.

Growing up, I attended a Mongolian public school. At first, everything seemed normal, and there was no serious bullying. The boys were silly, but that was expected. However, when I reached middle school, bullying became a significant issue. There were students who would take money from others, and fights between girls were common. Some fights started over relationships, while others were about dominance within the school. I was almost caught up in that environment, but thankfully, my friend—who was strong and confident—helped me navigate those challenges. I was very shy, and I found it difficult to talk to new people. If I knew someone for a while, I could open up, but speaking to teachers or asking questions was not easy for me.

When I was young, my mom enrolled me in various clubs, such as Mongolian dance and singing. I also played the piano and the violin. I appeared on television four or five times as a child. I started learning piano at the age of five and continued until COVID-19 disrupted my lessons. I participated in numerous competitions and often placed first, second, or third. In school, whenever there was a talent competition, I always took part and usually won because I was the only student who played the piano well.

In Mongolia, classrooms were crowded, often with thirty to forty students. We remained together from first grade until high school. However, in high school, students could choose a specific field of study, which determined their class placement for the last four years.

Before I entered seventh grade, my mom transferred me to a different school that was not public. Initially, I liked it because it offered Chinese and English classes, but it was far from home. I had to take a bus, which was a new experience for me. In Mongolia, most students walk to school, even from a young age. Taking the bus meant waking up at 5:00 a.m. and returning home around 5:00 p.m. I was the first student to board and the last to get off. Over time, I became stressed due to the long commute, schoolwork, and extracurricular activities. My mom eventually decided to transfer me back to my old school.

That year turned out to be great. I became close to my friends again, and we spent a lot of time together. On Women's Day, March 8, we watched movies and celebrated. After finishing middle school, I moved to the United States.

My parents and sister had long discussions before deciding to move. The decision was based on both personal reasons and my education. Living in Mongolia had its challenges, and my parents wanted better opportunities for my future.

Leaving was difficult. I had a cat for five years, but we had to leave him with my uncle. The night we left, my cat ran away and got lost, which made me incredibly sad. Saying goodbye to my grandparents was also painful because they were already in their mid-eighties, and I did not know if I would ever see them again. Leaving my extended family and friends was just as hard, especially since I had a big argument with my best friend before leaving. I told myself I would leave the past behind and start fresh, but I still carry those memories with me.

My first visit to the US was in 2017 for three months. Many people assumed I was an only child because my sister was elsewhere in the US, and I often felt lonely. My parents were always busy with work, so they got me a pet to keep me company.

Our journey to the US started with a flight to South Korea, then to Los Angeles, and finally to Chicago. My sister gave me the option to choose between California and Chicago, and I picked Chicago. However, when we arrived in Los Angeles, our flight to Chicago was delayed until 3:00 a.m. We were frustrated but had no choice but to wait.

Arriving in Chicago was a shock. I saw people from different cultures—Europeans, South Asians, and many others. It took time to adjust to the diversity. When we landed, my sister was there to welcome us. Seeing my niece for the first time was a joyful moment because I had always wanted a younger sibling, and she felt like one to me.

The first few days were tough. The time difference messed up my sleep schedule. I wanted to sleep during the day and stay awake at night. My sister told me to stay awake during the day to adjust, and eventually, I did. We first lived in an apartment with a pool; I spent every day swimming, which resulted in a deep tan.

After about three weeks, I started middle school again in eighth grade. The first day was overwhelming because I did not know where to go and ended up in the wrong class. A staff member helped me find my way. The first four months were especially hard because I only knew basic English—simple greetings and asking to use the restroom. Communicating with teachers and classmates was frustrating, but the students were kind and supportive. I made a good friend, Ala, who always listened patiently and helped me practice English.

I had played the violin in Mongolia, so I joined the school orchestra. Initially, the teacher thought I was a beginner, but when I played, she realized I was skilled enough to join the group. We participated in four competitions, and though I was nervous, being part of a team made me feel less alone. Reading violin notes was challenging at first because my classmates had years of experience, but I kept practicing.

Now, my life in the US is going well. I am learning English, solving problems, and improving myself. After school, I stay behind to do homework in the library or join clubs like the guitar club, the tennis club, and the crochet club. I sometimes bike or rollerblade around my neighborhood or walk with my mom in the evenings. On weekends, I used to take swimming lessons, but I paused because of the cold weather. I plan to join the swimming team in my junior year. I tried out this year but was not selected because I had not mastered freestyle swimming yet. However, I am determined to succeed next year.

For my future, I plan to go to college and pursue a career in the medical field—either as a nurse or a doctor. I have not decided which specialty yet, but I will figure it out in a few months. I want to make my parents proud because I am the first in my family to attend high school in the US. I will do my best to succeed and be a good daughter.

VIDEO LINKS

greencardvoices.org/speakers/gereltuya-bayarmagnai

EUROPE
Kyiv,
Ukraine

Yelyzaveta (Lisa) Rozhkova

Born: Kyiv, Ukraine

"AS A UKRAINIAN, I CARRY VALUES THAT CAN HELP BUILD A BRIDGE—ECONOMIC, CULTURAL, AND SPIRITUAL—BETWEEN OUR COUNTRIES AND ENABLE THEM BOTH TO THRIVE."

I would say that the first explosion changed everything. I did not realize how happy my life was before. I was born at the beginning of 2008, in the magical 1,500-year-old capital of Ukraine. I am talking about Kyiv—my beloved city.

I became the fourth child in my close-knit family, and two years later my brother was born. A few years later, our loyal beagle joined the family. We named him Steve—a rare name in Ukraine, but I loved the sound of it. He is the most loyal friend I ever had. I have a huge family for Ukraine, which has provided me with lifelong childhood memories.

We lived in a big, bright, and beautiful apartment on the eighteenth floor in the center of the city. Often on the weekends, we liked to visit my grandparents, who had a house in the suburbs. They had a big, beautiful garden, where we picked various berries and fruits that my grandma would use to make delicious dishes. They looked forward to our visits.

I especially looked forward to winter holidays, which were filled with national and family traditions. My favorite was Christmas. My mom would make twelve meatless holiday dishes that symbolized the twelve apostles. One of my favorite dishes is kutya, which we usually eat as a dessert after all the main dishes. We would also wait for the first star to appear, symbolizing the birth of Jesus.

I went to school and had a lot of friends. In the eighth grade, I enrolled in Kyiv's top liberal arts lyceum. There was also a formal dress code—I had to keep my hair tied up and wear formal clothing. No jeans, crop tops, or sweatpants. Since I have always been a creator, whose love of the arts is always growing, I continued playing piano (which I started at age four); learned various dance styles (from ballet to break dancing); and performed on stage. My first role was alongside my mom. Just a few years later, I auditioned and was invited to join a professional theater company.

This idyllic childhood was interrupted the morning I woke up to the sound of sirens. At first I thought it was just a drill. But then my mom came in and calmly said that we needed to get dressed and go down to the underground parking garage—it became our bomb shelter because Russia had attacked us. Just like that, the peaceful sky was covered with dark clouds of missiles and aircraft. It was terrifying. But this invasion strengthened and united us.

So many of my friends left for their safety, but we did not want to leave because not all of our family members could go with us. Leaving meant that our family would have to split apart. It was a very hard decision. We could not imagine our lives without our loved ones, thousands of kilometers away from our home.

After the war started, we did not know whether to leave. After a year, we realized that our turn to leave had come too. Many of my friends had already left, and before the New Year, while we were preparing food, the loudest explosion I had ever heard happened. It was very close to my house. Everyone just froze. We did not move. And after that, we ran into the hallway of our apartment.

It was time to leave. We thought it would be for just a few months, to get a break from the constant attacks and breathe without war. Then, our friends who had been living in the US for over twenty years offered to sponsor us, so we could see what life was like without sirens, explosions, and attacks.

We made the final decision at the last moment. We bought tickets, packed a few things, and left. Since the sky over Ukraine was closed to civilian flights, we had to start our journey by train. Our entire family came to see us off. My mom cried. It was extremely hard, and none of us wanted to leave. After we crossed the border, my mom, my younger brother, and I transferred to a local train and reached the capital of Poland. Then, we finally boarded the plane that took us to Chicago on February 26, 2023. Our plane trip to the US took about twelve hours.

It was late at night, and from the plane, I saw countless lights illuminating Chicago. It was beautiful. When we landed, I could finally breathe. It was simultaneously exciting and sad. Our friends were waiting for us at the airport. We had not seen them in years, so it was an incredible moment.

The first few months were incredibly hard. We were exhausted from the war, living thousands of kilometers away from home and loved ones. For the first few days, we stayed in a hotel. My mom and I walked around the neighborhood and were impressed by the clean, tidy, beautiful houses. But there were not many people outside, which was strange after the chaotic streets of my home country. I was also surprised to see gray, fluffy, plump squirrels running around.

I soon discovered what a multicultural country this is. My mom could not find work at first because of the language barrier, so we lived with our friends. We did not have a car and had to borrow one. I did not go to school right away because it was the middle of the academic year, so I finished my freshman year online in my Ukrainian school and then started sophomore year here. My younger brother started school immediately, but there was no space for him on the iconic yellow school bus, so he had to walk.

The first time I went to school to take placement tests and complete paperwork, I was curious about the dress code. I wanted to know how students dressed so I could fit in. I was surprised—there was no dress code at all. Students wore pajama pants, sweatpants, crop tops, slippers, and fuzzy shoes. It was weird at first, but I got used to it quickly. Now, I even dress in a similar way sometimes. I also discovered garage sales. We bought our first mode of transportation at one—a secondhand bicycle. It was fun, and I liked it.

Things were looking up, and soon my mom found a job —but she had to give up the career she had spent her whole life building. The movie she acted in when we were in Ukraine was even nominated for an Oscar this year for Best International Feature Film, yet here, she works as a nanny. I found a job at a local coffee shop to support her and make her life easier. We bought a car, rented an apartment, and now enjoy our own space.

My brother and I had to change schools, because here, school districts are tied to where you live. It was hard leaving behind my friends, who I keep in touch with while making new ones. I also returned to my hobbies—I started playing piano again and joined a dance program at school. I volunteer at a Ukrainian church to raise funds for our army. I also volunteer at school—recently, we had a fundraiser to help buy Christmas gifts for disadvantaged families.

I am grateful to have this opportunity to study at this unique, extraordinary school, despite the challenge of starting over with new teachers, new requirements, and new expectations. This journey has helped me become an adaptable, resilient, and creative young woman. I believe these qualities can contribute fresh ideas to the US economy and business. The US has become an inseparable part of my life. No matter what the future holds, these experiences will forever enhance my journey.

Since I have been interacting with native speakers, my English has improved significantly. My primary goal at this moment is to achieve a quality education because I see it as a foundation for my future—both personally and socially. I finally started bonding with people who understand my inner conflict, and my life is now filled with interesting people who are really caring and patient with me. I am really grateful for this.

Although my country faces significant challenges, I feel that together, it will be much easier to overcome them and make a positive impact on both of our nations. As a Ukrainian, I carry values that can help build a bridge—economic, cultural, and spiritual—between our countries and enable them both to thrive.

VIDEO LINKS

greencardvoices.org/speakers/yelyzaveta-rozhkova

SOUTH AMERICA
Colombia

Yohana

Born: Colombia

"LIFE IS BETTER WHEN YOU HAVE FAMILY AND FRIENDS; IT IS AN IMPORTANT THING."

My life in Colombia was nice, peaceful, and amazing. I lived in one of the most beautiful and picturesque cities in Colombia, with beaches, friendly people, and a great history. I will always feel fortunate to have been raised on the Colombian coast, a place where there is never a lack of good plans, charming places, delicious food, scorching sun, and music on every corner.

I remember that for months, my dad mentioned the idea of us going to the US for a better life; I was thinking, Why? That's so far for better opportunities. It turned out my brother had been recruited for an illegal group; for that reason, we had to leave for safety. I was nervous. Thanks to my dad's hard work for three months and the sale of our things, we were able to raise the money for the trip. We said goodbye to a few, but many only found out when we were in the US. The hardest thing of all was saying goodbye to the people I loved so much and knowing that I would not see them for a long time.

Thank God, our trip to the US went very well. I remember my mom and I went in January by plane; we left Colombia and finally arrived in Chicago. It was so cold, and I had never seen snow before. My skin, my hair, and I were freezing.

When my mom and I arrived, we were able to reunite with my dad. Our first month there, February 2024, my dad did not have a job, and it was hard. We gave thanks to God for blessing us with an opportunity to stay with friends of our family in Chicago.

Life here in the US was so different because I could get up later to go to school, which was a dream come true—in Colombia, we are very early risers. Most of my classes at the beginning were all in English, which scared me a little, but I had the help of my teachers and classmates to adapt.

Since I was born and raised in Colombia and the weather there is so hot, when I arrived here in the winter, the cold weather was so cruel. Now my family has adapted and we are close. That is amazing, because life is better when you have family and friends; it is an important thing. With my friends, I try to go out as much as I can to get to know the city. They are good company and have made my life here more enjoyable.

For the future, I want to speak better English. I want to be able to express myself freely and eventually become a doctor. I would also like to help my community through volunteer work. In the future, when I return to my homeland, I want to feel proud of the things I have done and have my head held high. I would like to go back to buy an arepa de huevo and have the sun of Colombia smile at me.

VIDEO LINKS

greencardvoices.org/speakers/yohana

AFRICA
Kigoma,
Tanzania

Akili Dieudonne

Born: Kigoma, Tanzania

"IT'S LIKE BEING BORN AGAIN, BUT IN A WORLD THAT EXPECTS YOU TO RUN BEFORE YOU CAN CRAWL."

I was born in the Kigoma Refugee Camp in Tanzania. My parents were born in Congo and fled to Tanzania in 1996 because of the war. I lived with them in the camp for about seventeen years. Life there was not good. We lived in bad conditions, and education was very poor.

I played with my friends. We used to play soccer together, but we did not have a real ball. We had to use plastic bags. And we would get strings too. To make a ball, we sometimes took a condom. We would blow it up. When it popped, we had to take some plastic bags, cut them into strips with a knife, and then tie them together with rubber bands to make a ball again. If the condom popped, we could not play anymore until we found another one.

There was not much in the camp. The leader of the Kigoma Refugee Camp was called Makazi. Makazi was not good. He did not want people to move out of the camp. If you wanted to leave, you had to pay him. We were not free. If you had a bike or a motorcycle, they would come and take it from you. If you built a nice house, they would come and destroy it, break it down to the ground. If you had your own clothing store, phone store, or any market, they would come at night wearing masks. They would rob you. Sometimes they would even shoot people if they refused to give their SIM card passwords. We did not have banks, so people kept money on their SIM cards. If you did not give your password, they would shoot. The police did not do anything to help. We were all scared all the time. It was hard.

Makazi did not want people in the camp to have any business or livestock, like beef and chicken. People get angry because it was too much, and they would protest. There was no good health care. People died too much. If you wanted to have surgery, you could not get a surgery. There were no medicine pills. There were a lot of diseases, like malaria.

One day, someone came running to tell me they had put my name on the wall. I went to see, and yes, my name was there! They had the selection date and everything. I had to go for a check-up to see if I had malaria or if I was sick. If you were sick, you could not go to America. They told us, "Your travel is being canceled. So wait for us, we'll give you the day when you'll travel to America." After one month, they called us.

Someone was running and shouting, "Akili! Akili!" When I saw my name on the wall, I said, "Weeeee!" I could not believe it. I had to go and check by myself. When I saw it, I said, "Oh my God, I'm going to America!" I was so happy, and my friends were so happy too. But I was sad because I was leaving my childhood friends. We were crying together because we could not hope to meet again one day. I was so excited because everybody wanted to go to America. It was everyone's dream, including mine, because life was so hard in the camp. My dreams were about to come true, because there in America, there were a lot of opportunities, a lot of support, good education, good work, and good health care.

When I got back home, I saw my mom too was happy because she had heard that we would go to America. My mom was telling me that I have to call my grandma and my aunties, because they live in America. She told me to tell them we would need money to shop for clothes, shoes, and suitcases. They were so happy because we had not seen each other for a long time.

We had to take a bus from the camp to a place called Kasulu. We stayed there for about two weeks. They checked us again for malaria and other sicknesses, telling us we could not go to America if we had malaria or any diseases.

I was scared because I had a fever. I woke up at night and ran around trying to make myself feel better. In the morning, a doctor checked me and said, "You have a fever." I told her that it was the sun, and she said, "Okay, you passed." My mom was looking at me, and she was nervous because she felt like we would stay there again. That is why she was telling me, "Please be strong." I said, "Okay, okay," even though I was scared. I stayed strong because of her.

We left the fence and boarded the bus. There was someone who called names to get on the bus; after calling everybody else, they called us. From there, we went to a small airport. In the airport, we had to be in a line and walk slowly, and the guards were checking our suitcases again before we went on the plane. Our suitcases had too many kilograms, so we had to take out some of our clothes because the plane was small. But for me, I was so happy because it was my first time seeing an airplane in my life.

The plane was not big, because we had to fly to Dar es Salaam. You could not go by bus; you had to take the airplane. We moved to Dar es Salaam.

It was about a two- or three-hour flight. When we got there, they checked us again. Everything was good. They gave us food, told us to take a shower there, and showed us where the bathroom was and where we would sleep. We stayed there for five hours. They said, "You will fly soon."

At 2:00 p.m., we boarded the plane to America. It was my first time on a real airplane, and I was so excited! Some workers from the International Organization for Migration traveled with us to help because we did not know English. They helped us with passports and anything else we needed.

Then we flew to Turkey. We stayed there about two hours. Then we boarded a bigger airplane to Chicago. I was so happy because it was my first time on a big airplane. There were about 500 people on that flight! Everything felt new to me. Every time I looked out the window and saw the sky, I asked, Is it me? It is me!

We were hungry; they came and asked us what we wanted, but we did not say anything because we did not know how to speak English. They gave their food to us. My mom and little sister did not like the airplane food. For them, it was hard. For me, it was fine because I was used to eating anything.

Using the bathroom on the airplane was really difficult for me; I did not know how to open the bathroom doors because it was a new thing. In the bathrooms in my camp, we put some clothes tied around a stick, and if you wanted to go to the bathroom, you had to clap to get in. That is why in the airplane, we did not understand how the bathroom worked, because in my country using the bathroom is easy. That is why I did not use the bathroom in the airplane during the whole trip! Because of that, after arriving, I did not go to the bathroom for almost two weeks. My stomach hurt so much because I was eating too much new food that was mixing with the old food.

When we landed in Chicago, our family, who were already here, came to welcome us at the airport. We were so happy to see them. We were taking pictures at the airport and singing some songs to thank God because we had arrived safely in America. They took me and my parents from the airport to show us our house, because they came to the US before us. Everything was ready. In the house, there was food, and they would make more food for us. It was beautiful, our house. They were asking, "How was your travel? How was the camp?"

When it was morning, I walked outside. I was amazed by everything like trains, tall buildings, cars. I did not see that before in the camp—in the camp, the biggest transportation we saw was bicycles.

At first I was worried; it was making me miss a lot of things from camp. I was missing farming, playing with friends, the feeling of being able to talk to people. In my camp, we could talk to anyone. But in America, you cannot talk to anyone if you do not know them. That is why I was feeling bored and I remembered my camp a lot.

In America, the first time I saw snow, I was confused and started saying, "What is this?! Where does it come from?!" I was touching it because I could feel it hit me. But it was not what I was thinking. That day was cold and strange. When I came back to my house, my brother was there and told me, "I want to go outside with you"; then we went downtown. That day was my first time going downtown; I was shocked and I was so confused. I saw so many people walking there, so many buildings, so many cars. I felt like the buildings would come and fall on me.

My brother took me to try some American food. I had not eaten American food before. That was my first time, and I was feeling so good. I was enjoying that day, feeling like I was in Heaven. After finishing, we went back home, and he showed me how to take a shower. I did not know how to open the shower handle for the water to come. He showed me how can you could have cold water and how you can have hot water.

I have now been here for about a year and a half. One of the biggest opportunities I got was through my father's friend. He introduced me to a sponsor. She helped me join Chicago City Soccer Club. I was telling him how I love soccer. It is my dream because I want to be a professional soccer player. Now, I feel like everything is possible. In America there are a lot of opportunities. When it was my first time to go play soccer, it was too hard to talk to my teammates because of the language. They would speak English, and for me it was hard to speak English.

Right now, I am a senior in high school. I am almost done. I am really happy. After school, I plan to go to college and play soccer there. I want my dream to come true. In my house, I live with my mom, my stepfather, and my little sister. We have four people in the house. On weekends, I go to the beach, play soccer, or play video games with my friends at my house.

In the future, the one thing I would like to learn about is being a police officer. But my mom says she does not want me to be a police officer. She wanted to study nursing, so now I have to study to be a nurse. For now, I want to focus on my soccer dream. I believe I am going to make it and reach my goal. If I reach my goal, I will buy my house and buy my favorite car, make my mom happy, and do whatever I want to do in my life.

VIDEO LINKS

greencardvoices.org/speakers/akili-dieudonne

Mixed Media
ASIA
Seoul,
South Korea

Yeseo (Esther) Jee

Born: Seoul, South Korea

"KOREA IS A SMALL COUNTRY, BUT I WANT PEOPLE FROM THERE TO HAVE A STRONG INFLUENCE IN THE WORLD."

I was born in Seoul. My life was pretty simple, because I never moved; I lived in the same city until my middle school. I went to elementary school with my kindergarten friends, and I went to the same middle school with my elementary school friends, so it was pretty easy.

It was easy to transition from elementary to middle school, and there were a lot of apartments, so I usually walked to school. I usually took a walk with my friends every day. It took ten minutes to get to school. My school had seven classes. I stayed in the same class until the eighth period, and different teachers came to the classroom, so my classmates never changed throughout the year.

I had a younger sister, but she and I went to different middle schools because my house was between two middle school areas. I went to the left area, and my sister went to the right area. I usually did not talk to my younger sister while I was in Korea. I did not meet her alone a lot. I met her after I went to Suhak Hakwon, a math academy with tutors, where I learned math and English. I was with my tutor until 10:00 p.m., and I took a walk afterward. I came back home at around 11:00 p.m.

At school, they did not give us a lot of homework, but Suhak Hakwon gave us a lot of homework. I usually did the homework from the tutor during lunch at school; I made friends through tutor things too, because I usually spent a lot of time there.

There were all sorts of things to do hanging out in Korea. There was a photobooth for like two dollars, and I usually took a photo with my friends there when we hung out. Sometimes I went to the playground and just played tag.

I found out I was going to be moving to the US when I was in eighth grade. When I heard that I was going to the US, I was surprised, and I felt like I was in a dream. I told my friends, and then a few of my friends cried.

My dad told me that he had been posted to the US because not enough people were working during COVID-19, so his company sent him overseas. Before he decided to go to the US, he asked my family if he should; everyone said yes, except my younger sister. I thought my English could get better easily and quickly when I came to the US, so I said yes. My mom and grandparents thought that it would improve my education. My sister was scared of losing and being separated from her friends. She said no, and refused to give in.

I had to get a visa and green card to come to the US, and I had to learn English because I was not good at it. When I was in Korea, one time, I got six out of 100 in English. I studied English for a year before I came to the US; I also had to give up my friendships. It does not mean we are not friends anymore, but it is hard to text and see them. To them, I feel like I became an "old" friend.

I did not travel or move much before leaving Seoul. My parents helped me pack my suitcase, and I came to the US with them. They handled everything, taught me how to go through the airport, and took care of everything for me.

We moved to Chicago because of my dad's company, so we did not get to choose the city. However, my parents chose this specific area because of its good education system. They wanted me to meet a lot of people and make friends here.

When I arrived, I noticed the air was really dry. I think it is because Korea is humid. I was excited to move into a bigger house. In Korea, almost everyone lives in apartments, and most houses have only one floor. In the US, I moved into a two-story house, which made me really excited.

I arrived during summer break in June 2022, so for two months, I did not go to school. I just played games with my friends in Korea. I stayed up all night and slept in the morning, so it still felt like I was in Korea. However, when school started, I got really nervous about speaking English with people. They spoke way faster than I expected.

In Korea, the school system is different. There are six years of elementary school, three years of middle school, and three years of high school. When I moved to the US, I was supposed to be in tenth grade, but I had to start ninth grade again and only did it for three months. Choosing my own schedule was hard because, in Korea, everyone has the same schedule. However, I was excited that I could take art class every day. In Korea, we only had art class once or twice a week.

English was the hardest subject here, especially because I had to learn everything in that language. I did not understand anything at first, so I got a

Korean tutor to help me. It took time because I had to translate everything into English. Also, the time we had for tests felt way too short because I had to read every question in English.

I liked hanging out with my friends in Korea, but when I first moved here, I did not have any friends. I was scared to talk to people, so I felt really lonely. At first, I really wanted to go back to Korea.

After moving here, I picked up a lot of new hobbies. I started playing guitar and baking desserts. There were not many restaurants here, so I started cooking for myself. In Korea, I never had a chance to play guitar, but when I saw that my school offered a guitar class, I took it and got really into it. I also loved drawing in Korea, but I started drawing even more here. Since I had art class every day, I drew all the time.

I feel like my family got closer after moving to the US. I started spending more time with my sister. At first, she felt just as lonely as I did, so we started talking more. We even got into the same hobby—playing Roblox—so we often played together. In the US, school ends at 3:30 p.m., so I had time to hang out with my friends or my sister. In Korea, I had tutoring until 10:00 p.m. and did not get home until 11:00 p.m. I did not have time to play games or hang out with friends except on weekends.

In the future, I want to be famous, especially in art. My sister and I have talked about starting a clothing brand together. I want to make my name known so that even after I die, people will remember me. I also want other people like me—immigrants from Korea—to become successful. Korea is a small country, but I want people from there to have a strong influence in the world.

VIDEO LINKS

greencardvoices.org/speakers/

AFRICA
Nigeria

Fay

Born: Nigeria

"I LEARNED THAT I AM NOT JUST NIGERIAN. I AM ALSO BLACK."

I was born in Nigeria. I live with my mom. We were very family oriented, in a way; everybody lived close to each other. I remember that we lived in my house my dad built, and we would all eat together. It was me, my mom, my grandma, and my five siblings. Our school was down the street from us. My cousins lived six minutes away from us; we lived in a very tight-knit community.

I remember when my dad would take us on a road trip back to our home state and my siblings and cousins would crowd into the same car together. We would sit on each other's laps to make space. We would listen to music. After we arrived at our family's house where my grandma lives, we would go to the market with my grandma and help her sell food. I really enjoyed my time with everyone, and I would not trade it for the world. I also miss my dad's Christmas parties. My dad would throw a Christmas party to celebrate the end of the year; everyone in my family and in the community would be in our house until the next day.

My dad and I landed in the United States in 2017. We had to wait for a while; after that, we went out. I had never seen snow before, never even heard about it. It was a shocking experience. We had somebody waiting for us at the summit. Our travel agent connected with somebody, and we stayed there for about a month before moving to Oklahoma. During that time, McDonald's was the first meal I ever had in America. On the plane, I did not eat at all. My dad was terrified because I am a picky eater.

After the first month, we took a bus to Oklahoma. My father was terrified because again I would not eat. We had a stopover somewhere; during the stop, there was a little shop where my dad got us sandwiches, but I refused to eat for the whole three-day bus ride. My father was terrified, and it was still snowing. Finally, we got to my aunt's house.

The biggest obstacle for me was people thinking I did not understand English. It is not my second language, but I learned it at the same time I learned

Yoruba; they went hand in hand, because I went to a Yoruba school where we only spoke English. The cultural change was different; the kids just talked to teachers, however, and I was not used to them being so open. I think the opportunities were not really there for me until I got to high school, because I was a shy kid in middle school.

When I got to high school, that was my opportunity to shine. I joined clubs and got to understand how different I am from people. You are not going to find somebody who is the exact same as the next person, so that was a whole opportunity itself. The people I were around also liked learning new things. That got me into social work and social justice. It would be different for everybody else, because I had to give up family in a way—after I moved here, everybody I knew was in Nigeria. I did not have anyone to talk to. My entire life was back home, and I had to learn to build new relationships. We did not come as a family, and my dad had left when I was in Oklahoma. He went back home with my mom, because he had five kids he needed to support.

After I moved to Chicago, my mom joined me with my siblings. My dad is in the UK, and two of my siblings are still in Nigeria. That is my biggest regret, because my family is split, and having them back home while we are all here just does not sit right with me.

At school, I have helped build communities in a way. I serve as a student representative on our school's council and hold a role in the student business leadership organization. I also cheerlead and am a soccer player. I am part of different clubs, including a youth social justice organization and a cultural affinity group at my school. Everyone connects to one another. I built a community in high school, and I hope I left a mark in some way. I want to build communities everywhere I go.

I love talking to people, so being able to understand where they come from and the reasons they do things is a really important thing for me. I want to build communities wherever I go. I want to become a lawyer. I am going into accounting first. After I become an accountant, I am going to go into tax law and become a lawyer.

I think a challenge for me in the US was understanding the difference between African American and African. I grew up in Nigeria, where everything is just about tribe. But when I got here, I learned that I am not just Nigerian. I am also Black. I love that, because I also had to learn about my rich history and how I would be perceived by people. It was a challenge at first, but I got to understand it more.

VIDEO LINKS

greencardvoices.org/speakers/fay

ASIA
Ulaanbaatar,
Mongolia

Bayarmagnai (Bay) Batochir

Born: Ulaanbaatar, Mongolia

"I WORRIED PEOPLE WERE JUDGING ME JUST FOR BEING ASIAN. BUT AFTER A WHILE, I REALIZED THAT THERE ARE SO MANY DIFFERENT PEOPLE HERE THAT NO ONE ACTUALLY CARED."

I was born in a small countryside town in Mongolia; my family moved to the city when I was just a month old. I grew up in Ulaanbaatar, the capital city, where about a third of the country's population lives. It is the most densely populated place in Mongolia, and honestly not the best in terms of quality of life—there is heavy air pollution, crowded streets, and traffic everywhere, kind of like downtown Los Angeles.

I have two younger sisters; one is seven and the other is eleven. Back in Mongolia, I went to school and played a lot of volleyball, but when I found out we were moving to the US, I started playing basketball because America is a basketball country.

The main reason we chose the US was that we had a lot of people we knew here. We followed them to Chicago and decided to settle here. Another big reason was my sister's medical condition—she has epilepsy, which causes seizures. The US has some of the best doctors and the most advanced medical technology, so it felt like the right choice. Education was also a big factor; the schools are better.

In Mongolia, we were considered upper class. My mom was a teacher, and my dad was a pilot, but here, their jobs are not as good as they were back home. Coming to the US meant giving up a lot—our homes, our cars, and my parents' careers.

The journey itself was not too bad. We took a thirteen-hour flight, since Mongolia and the US are basically on opposite sides of the world. I was used to flying because of my dad's job, but this was still a long trip. I had never left Mongolia before, so it was a big deal. When we arrived in Chicago in 2023, my parents' friends picked us up in Buffalo Grove, and we moved into an apartment near them. They helped us a lot—getting a car, finding a place to rent, and settling in.

My first hour in the US, I was so nervous. It was my first time seeing people from so many different countries—Indian, Mexican, Black, white. Everyone was so tall, and everything felt so different.

The first week and month were tough. I was scared of discrimination because of my race. I worried people were judging me just for being Asian. But after a while, I realized that there are so many different people here that no one actually cared. In Mongolia, we thought Americans were mostly racist toward nonwhite people, but so far, I have not experienced that here.

At first, we lived in an apartment because we did not own property here. But with the help of my parents' friends, we were able to get a car and find a good place to live.

Since I had just started playing basketball about a year or two ago, I could not make any teams. In the US, kids started playing sports at a very young age, so they were way ahead of me. School here was also much easier than in Mongolia—there is barely any homework!

When I first arrived in the US as a freshman in March, I could not go to school for about four months. Because of that, I ended up skipping ninth grade. Now I go to Stevenson High School. I had no idea how the American school system worked—what GPA was, how grading worked, or anything like that. One thing that surprised me was that teachers do not grade homework here, which was good news for me!

Another thing that was really different was the way classes worked. In Mongolia, students stay in one classroom, and the teachers move between classes. Here, students move from class to class, and the schedule is different every day. Also, in Mongolia, we study every subject—math, physics, biology, chemistry—all in one week, while in the US, we get to choose electives like art classes.

I miss my friends from Mongolia because we spent all day together in the same class, so we were really close. Here, even if you have friends, you might not see them at all during the school day, and it is harder to hang out outside of school. I like to play video games at home or play basketball with friends after school. Sometimes, I stay after school to hang out, but usually, I just go home.

My parents say they might go back to Mongolia in a few years. But they want me to finish college in the US first and then decide whether I want to stay here or return to Mongolia. My sisters are in school here too—one is in middle school, and the other is in elementary school. They are learning English quickly compared to how we learned it in Mongolia.

As for the future, I hope to start a successful business—either in the US or Mongolia, it does not really matter. I just want to be successful, and hopefully pretty rich.

VIDEO LINKS

greencardvoices.org/speakers/bayarmagnai-batochir

ASIA
Damascus,
Syria

Sebba Saad Allah

Born: Damascus, Syria **Raised:** Jordan

"I USED TO HEAR A LOT OF MUSICIANS ON THE STREET SINGING, PEOPLE WALKING AROUND, MERCHANTS WITH THEIR SMALL CARTS SELLING COOKIES AND JUICES, AND VISITORS COMING FROM OTHER LANDS OUTSIDE TO VISIT AND EXPLORE DAMASCUS."

I lived in Syria in a beautiful city called Damascus, the capital and one of the largest cities. When I was five years old, I used to walk around with my mom in the streets. I remember the beauty of my motherland. I used to smell the jasmine all around and kids playing soccer. I enjoyed it so much.

I used to hear a lot of musicians on the street singing, people walking around, merchants with their small carts selling cookies and juices, and visitors coming from other lands outside to visit and explore Damascus. I could see the love and peace all around. You feel that your own country is spreading love to you and others.

I love that we were very kind people to others, and I think everybody should have a chance to go and see the way Damascus is. It is a very large city filled with love, kindness, beautiful nature, and beautiful art. When I was in Syria, my dream was to live in the US because I used to remember when visitors would come to explore my country, and I wanted to be like them and discover their country.

In 2011, the Syrian civil war started, and it took a big part of my happiness. I had to live with no food or drinks, in a small tent, even though I used to live in a house that had three rooms, a beautiful backyard, and all of my family around me. In a second, I was alone with my mother, father, and brother. The only thing I used to hear was soldiers with their gunshots.

I was forced to leave my country and go to Jordan. That was the only choice I had. I, my mother, my father, and my brother had to leave. I lived in Jordan for six years. I liked the way I was living there, even though it was hard for me because I got bullied. I was called a Syrian girl who did not belong anywhere, and they were telling me to go back to my country. It was a second country for me, my homeland.

When I was informed that I had to come to Chicago, I did not want to leave. I did not want to start all over again because my family and I had built everything for six years—now we had to rebuild again. It was a very hard decision for me and my family. I was ten when I had to decide with my parents.

I had a lot of mixed feelings. I was thinking of my future, but also thinking of where I was right now. Am I going to get bullied again? Am I going to be in an environment that loves me? Am I going to be that girl who one day might go out and actually share her story?

My parents thought that coming to the US might help the way people saw me and give me a better education. I was informed that my airplane to Chicago would leave in 2019. I did not know anybody in the US. I had my uncle, but he lived far away.

The night before the flight, at 10:00 p.m., my mom said, "Let's go. We have to pack, we have to sell our stuff." The airplane was at four in the morning, so we had to leave. I was helping my mom pack everything. I was saying goodbye to my friends. I was just crying the whole time and did not want to go.

We got an Uber and headed to the airport. My aunt was there. She was saying goodbyes, and everybody was crying. I was the only one who did not want to cry, but I ended up crying. It was hard, because war had already taken half my family from me. I had to go to the US without my family. I had to be separated again.

I waited six hours at the airport for the airplane. The only thing I was thinking about was my new life, my future, and how I was going to be surrounded by many different cultures and religions. The US is a very big country that has a lot of different people from all around the world. I was nervous, thinking, What am I going to do? I was lost.

That was when the airplane landed; then I made it to Chicago. When I landed at the airport, it was sunny outside. I could see the view, I could see the cars, and I could see the people walking all around. I was happy and excited to explore life, but I was very afraid of getting bullied.

When I was at the airport, I was waiting for the Uber to pick us up. When we were in the Uber, I was looking all around. I was looking at the view, at the beautiful streets. It was really beautiful, like Jordan. I was just exploring, thinking, How am I going to be part of those people that are walking one day? Am I going to feel confident walking around? That is what I was thinking about.

The first couple of months living here in Chicago, I did not focus on school. I was focusing more on nature, the environment. When my mother told me that I had to go back to studying and finish my education, I did not want to give up on my dreams. I did not know how students were going to treat me. I did not know how students were going to talk to me. Were they going to call me names again?

The only thing I was thinking about was that I did not want to be in a school with different kids and students. That day, I went to my bed thinking to myself, I just don't want to give up. I gave up so much before that—I did not want to give up anymore.

I woke up in the morning and told my mom I was ready to go back to school and continue my education. The first day of school, I was welcomed. Students were welcoming me, being really nice to me, and saying, "You belong here."

I saw a huge difference between where I was living and the world I came from. I loved everybody. I made friends; I became so close to them, and I am still talking to them today.

One challenge I had was the language. It was really hard. I had to practice day and night. I used to go back home and stay up late practicing, reading, writing, even doing math for no reason, just to help me learn. It was a really hard challenge.

Also, I was focusing on my parents and my siblings. They cannot speak English. It was really hard. I was thinking about my family, how they were going to make money, how we were going to live here. Chicago is really expensive. But we were thinking more about the positive sides than the negative sides.

I just love that I belong to everybody here. Right now, I am in high school. I am a sophomore. Even though I am still facing some challenges today, I really like my life. I like to walk around a lot. I wake up early in the morning, make breakfast with my mom, put on different music, and enjoy the morning. I open the window and look at nature outside, how beautiful the weather is. Every time my mom has to go get some groceries, I go with her just so I can look around and get to know more about how life actually is.

I used to play volleyball, but then I had to stop because I found a job. I had to help my mother after we lost my father, who had cancer. I actually like my work right now. I became a busy girl. I like that. I wake up early in the morning, go to school, finish my school, go to work, and then end up going back home late sometimes. But I like it.

I want my future to be the same as it is right now. I did so many successful things in my life after leaving my homeland and Jordan. I want to work on my goals and work on the dreams I promised my dad before he passed away.

I just want my future to be very peaceful. I do not want anything to happen, so I am rebuilding everything all over again. I just want to continue where I am right now. I want to feel loved. I want my family to feel loved. I want my siblings to grow up around me. Even though they are young right now and they do not know anything yet, they are exploring life. I want to go to college and become a surgeon or doctor.

VIDEO LINKS

greencardvoices.org/speakers/sebba-saad-allah

CALIFORNIA
1994
LOS ANGELE
SOUTH AMERICA
Venezuela

Douglas

Born: Venezuela **Raised:** Chile

"I WOULD LIKE TO BE ABLE TO REPRESENT MY COUNTRY FROM HERE—LET THEM KNOW THAT WE CAN MAKE A DIFFERENCE. NO MATTER HOW SMALL THAT DIFFERENCE IS, WE CAN BE SOMEONE BIG."

My life in Venezuela was so good. I lived with my mom, my dad, and my brother. In 2013, the supply of goods was not very strong. There were shortages of all kinds of food—for example, flour, rice, spaghetti, and other things. It was very difficult to survive. My dad protested for a better situation for our country, for our future. He wanted to secure a better life for me and my brother so we would not get lost in what was happening.

One day, my dad went out to protest. He never came back after that day. From what I know, word of his death was published in a newspaper by the police. The police published in the newspaper that a man had been murdered in the trunk of a car. They did not say why. They just said that. After that day, my life was not normal. My mom and my grandpa were constantly threatened because of the protests that my dad did. He wanted to make a difference in the country so that we would not continue to live like that. When my little brother was born, my dad was not with us anymore. My mom had to leave the university to support us. She could not afford it. My grandpa was the only one supporting us.

After a while, my mom was able to raise some money and decided to leave the country. But she did not have enough money for my brother and sister. We had to stay in Venezuela with my grandpa while my mom went to start a new life. We were recognized in our neighborhood because of our dad. My mom traveled to Chile, promising that one day we would go with her.

In 2021, my brother and I traveled to Chile. When we arrived in Chile, we were happy because we were finally going to leave Venezuela. Even though my mom was out of the country, she was being threatened by messages. She tried to hide it from me, but I understood the situation she was going through. I grew up with that, but I could never talk about it or explain it to anyone.

While in Chile, my mom found a new partner with whom she had a son. Around that time, there was a lot of resentment, hatred, and discrimination that started against Venezuelans. Due to that, my mom lost her job and their landlord asked them to evict the house. They lived with another family for a month and then decided to move to the United States because of the economic instability. It was challenging for my mom to find a new job and a place for us to live.

My mom decided to come to the United States because she said we needed a better future, and that we needed to move forward so that our dad's death would not be in vain. She did not want us to end up like him because of the country, because of how it is. When we were going to travel to the United States, they told us the borders were closing. But we already had everything done. We had suitcases, we had luggage.

We were staying at a friend of my mom's when she decided to go to Venezuela again. She said it had been a while; maybe the police would not remember anymore and would not come after her. She also said that by being in Venezuela, we were closer to traveling to the United States when we could travel again.

We traveled by bus because we did not have passports; renewing them cost a lot of money, and we did not have that much. The trips were very difficult. There were very few times we could sleep, and we always had to be on the bus.

When we arrived in Venezuela, we decided to spend Christmas and stay for three months. When February arrived, we would go to the United States, or, if the border was still closed, we would have to return to Chile or another country. My mother knew that Venezuela was not a stable country and that protests would continue. Still, in those three months that we were in Venezuela, we were enjoying ourselves. I was visiting all my family, friends that I had not seen in a long time. We traveled to the beach. We went to the park. We played soccer.

But apart from all that, one day the police came to my house, knocking on the door. They were looking for my mother for no reason. They took her away. They detained her for a whole day. They took money that she had saved to move to another house because we lived in my grandfather's house. They did not give any explanation of why; they simply told her that she was a terrorist because my dad had protested. My dad had died about nine years ago, and they kept tormenting us with the same things. That night, I could not sleep well because my mother was not at home. My three brothers and I were at home.

My grandfather did not know what to do.

After losing all that money, my mom decided that we were not going to be in Venezuela anymore. She told us that we had to travel to the United States because we needed to have a better future. There would not be anything for us in Venezuela. It was not good anymore.

My mom told me, the oldest son, that she did not have enough money to take us everywhere. There were four of us kids, along with her and her husband. We had a talk with my brothers, my mother, and my stepdad. In that talk, she told us that we could not all go; we had to separate from my two brothers, who are still in Venezuela, who still live there with my grandfather. My brothers understood the reasons we needed to leave, because they also knew that the cause of all this was my dad's death; that was why they accused my mother, because they had nothing to say against us. After all, we were innocent kids, and we did not know.

We walked for seven days to get to a city in Mexico that was very close to the border. By the time we were in Mexico, my mom had no money left, so she had to borrow a lot of money to be able to get there. Then a cousin of hers, who lives in Mexico, sent her money to go stay at her house for a while. We stayed at her house for a month in April 2022.

We then went to the border to turn ourselves in to immigration, waiting for the buses to arrive so they could take us through. There they changed our clothes, because the clothes we were wearing were all wet and damaged from crossing the Rio Grande.

When I arrived in the US, I went to a refugee center in San Pedro, Texas, for a day. It was a very big center. There were many people there. There was no space, and people would have to sleep on the floor with a sheet—they could not sleep on the beds because they were occupied by the people who travelled with small children. We did not have any money or anywhere to stay. Then they gave us the plane tickets to come to Chicago.

When I arrived in Chicago, everything was different. The city is beautiful. The people were different. People are good. They are no longer mean to us. At first it was hard for me to adapt to school, because I was still thinking about my brother and sister and what would happen to them, because they are still in Venezuela. But I also thought about what would become of me if I were there. My younger brother, who was born in Chile, came, along with my mom's husband. But my brother and sister stayed behind in Venezuela. We came here promising them that one day they would come here with us. Now, my mother is starting to do better at work, but we still have difficulties with everything. We are already collecting money to get passports for my brother and sister, to see if we can bring them to America.

It has been almost two years since I came to Chicago. I have been studying, learning since the first day I got here, to be able to understand the language. At first it was very difficult for me. I could not talk to anyone. I was just sitting alone because people did not understand me, and I did not understand them. Now, I go to school, and I am very happy. I can understand the language a little more. It is a little more difficult for me to pronounce, but it is not the same as when I first arrived. I feel better; I am sure that I am going to meet my brothers again, and that I can secure my future here in this country.

I would like to study finance because I have always been passionate about mathematics since I was little. Although it is a bit complicated here, I have always been fascinated by mathematics. It has always been my favorite subject. I would like to be able to represent my country from here—let them know that we can make a difference. No matter how small that difference is, we can be someone big.

VIDEO LINKS

greencardvoices.org/speakers/douglas

ASIA
Kuala Lumpur,
Malaysia

Hamidah Binti Mohamad Ikbal

Born: Kuala Lumpur, Malaysia

"EVEN WHEN WE CAME TO THE US WITH IDENTIFICATION AND ALL THE DOCUMENTS, THEY STILL LABELED US AS IMMIGRANTS."

I was born in Kuala Lumpur, Malaysia. My family is very diverse. We have all kinds of cultures in my family, but overall, it is Burmese, Rohingya, and Malaysian.

On my mom's side, my grandparents had a love marriage. My grandma was very stubborn and did not want to admit that she liked my grandpa, but they had a very strong bond in our home. My mom was very happy with their marriage until my grandma died later on. Then she ended up having step-siblings and a stepmother. She was still happy with them, but she was a bit more distant from her family. On my dad's side, my grandparents had an arranged marriage, and that also led to my parents' being arranged.

In Malaysia, from the stories my sister has told me, we had a farm in our backyard. My parents loved to grow plants and even harvest them. From the stories my sister has told me, it feels more like home there than it has been here. It feels more normal there, especially since everything was fresh in Myanmar and Malaysia. As soon as they caught the fish, they cooked it. As soon as they grew the berry or the fruit, they ate it, even off the tree branch. It was that fresh, and hearing the stories makes me want to go back there. It makes me think how life would be if I were actually there.

We moved to Malaysia because of my dad's job, and we stayed there for fifteen years. My dad bought a house and a car. We had a good life there, but the decision to stay was off and on. We started having financial problems, and there was not a good overall education system. Also, because the government and military were taking control in Malaysia, it was not a place where a lot of people wanted to be. So we moved to the United States for a better education, a better life, and a better income.

When we came to the US, it was not an easy process at all. There were a lot of steps. We needed identification cards. We needed a lot of documents. We could not just come here with random papers, because America would not accept us. Even when we came to the US with identification and all the documents, they still labeled us as immigrants.

I have five siblings: one older sister, three older brothers, and one younger brother. My younger brother was born when we came to the US. He was born a month before my birthday, so it was kind of like my birthday gift.

Coming to the United States was extremely hard because we had to adjust to the weather—in Malaysia, it is really hot and rainy and not cold at all. We had to adjust to the weird foods, especially with our taste buds and all the processed foods. We also had to adjust to people and the way they looked at us. To this day, it makes my family kind of weird. It makes us feel like we do not belong, even though sometimes we do.

We had a relative here at one point—he moved before us and adapted to the US before we did. When we came to the US, he showed us how everything runs, like the taxes, the food, the people, everything, even the language. He showed us a community center. The person in charge is named Bob, so it's called the Bob Center. He helped us get into schools. He helped us get materials. He was an amazing person, and so was his wife. They helped us get comfortable and feel more at home, like it was our home here.

When we came to America, the language was a big obstacle that my family had to go through. My siblings only knew a little bit because of the classes they took in Malaysia, and my parents knew none—they grew up speaking their own language, so they had absolutely no clue how to talk to others in English.

Since I am a Muslim, the food options here were very narrow, and we could not eat a lot of the stuff because it contained pork or gelatin. America people love their dogs, but seeing all the dogs and seeing people eat pork and processed foods made us wonder if things like that were like normal here. It was a lot, and it was very overwhelming with all the changes. Overall, it was very uncomfortable for my whole family.

One little thing about Myanmar is that everyone is of the same race, the same people. Everyone knows each other, even if they live really far away. Even in Malaysia, like in the same neighborhood, everyone knows each other. Coming to this new place, no one knew anyone, and we were completely brand-new. Not knowing any friends, any people I could trust in, really overwhelmed me; I did not really feel comfortable at all, and I just wanted to go back to my family.

When we came to America, there were a lot of opportunities. We had a better financial state. We bought a house here, and we had cars. We got better education than we could have ever gotten in Malaysia or Myanmar, especially with the war coming on. If we decided to go back, we would not be able to be in the same state as we are here in the US.

Looking back on my life, I gave up my culture. I gave up who I felt I was before I came here. Even though I was very little, I had a sense of who I was; when I came here, I had to change everything, because people either were really racist and did not want to accept the part of me that I already accepted, or just chose not to know the stuff about me that was related to my culture and religion.

During preschool and elementary school, I did not know anyone, and I was pretty much the loner kid in class. Everyone found a friend; I was the only one in the corner of the room or the playground just playing with myself, because I did not really know anyone, and was not comfortable talking to people I did not find familiar.

But toward middle school, I started finding people I actually liked and felt comfortable around. There were more Asian kids who started coming in. And even though they were also new, I knew how they felt, and I just was really happy to have that connection with other people. Overall, in middle school, I had an amazing bond with everyone there.

Starting high school was hard because I had to restart with my friends. I had to restart my bonds, especially since my friends went to different schools and we did not see each other at all. But there were a lot of good things as well. I got into all honors classes. I am on a path to a successful job and career, hopefully.

My favorite subject is math. I just love the challenge that it gives me whenever I work on math problems or help my classmates with them if they do not understand. My favorite sports are badminton and volleyball, and I also play soccer. My hobbies include baking and cooking. I also love playing hockey in my free time. I have a lot of hobbies, and I can't really pinpoint just one of them. I love cooking and baking because they bring people together, and I can give something that I love to someone else and have them enjoy it.

On February 2025, I became a naturalized citizen. I have been here for ten years now. I have been doing the Pledge of Allegiance every day since elementary school, because it was kind of like a requirement. Everyone was doing it. But that point just felt really weird—like I'm a person here, I'm an actual citizen now. I felt more normal; still, even though I grew up here, people still see me as an unordinary and an immigrant, even though I tried changing that.

Looking ahead, I want to contribute to my new community in meaningful ways. I want to build a life that honors my parents' sacrifices and my own dreams. I am planning on getting a master's degree, then getting a good and steady job that would also make me really happy. I have also been planning on moving with my friends and living a life that I dream about every single day for the last ten years. I want to give back to the country that gave us a new start, while still remembering and honoring the roots I came from.

VIDEO LINKS

greencardvoices.org/speakers/hamidah-binti-mohamad-ikbal

ASIA
Goyang,
South Korea

Daeyun Lee

Born: Goyang, South Korea

"I WANT TO GIVE HOPE TO OTHERS WHO ARE IMMIGRATING TO THE US OR JUST STRUGGLING WITH SOMETHING NEW. I WANT TO SHOW THEM THAT IF I CAN DO IT, THEY CAN TOO."

In South Korea, I was an only child, but I had five cousins. My family did not have any pets, and every day was pretty much the same. School was routine, and I had a lot of friends. The culture in South Korea is a little different from here. We have a unique way of speaking depending on age—different language styles for people the same age and for elders. That was something that felt a little strange.

I did not move around much in Korea. My daily schedule was simple: school, extra study, and home. That was my routine every day. I was born in a small town called Pungsan just west of Goyang City, which is a town northwest of Seoul, the capital city. It was a simple life with less traffic, and a beautiful park that I used to visit. It had a lake, and we could go for a walk or bike around it.

It has been about four months since my father first told me we were moving to the US. It happened during dinner. My father came home and casually asked, "How do you feel about the US?" I answered, "Oh, it sounds good," thinking he was asking about a vacation. But then he said, "No, we are moving to the US." That was shocking because I had always assumed I would live in Korea forever. After five minutes of processing, I just thought, "Oh, I'm going to the US." I did not have a strong emotional reaction at that moment. I told my friends, "Guys, I'm moving to the US," and that was that.

I had to give up time with my friends in South Korea because I needed to focus on studying English. Everything was in English, so I had to learn a lot of vocabulary and also study American culture. Even small things, like saying "Bless you" when someone sneezes, were new to me.

My father left a few months before us. At home in Korea, we only kept the essential furniture for living, so there was not much to pack. I packed my books and clothes but left behind old furniture like my desk and chairs since I would not need them anymore. We did not sell our house because we felt it was not necessary, so it is still ours.

We moved to Chicago because of my father's job. His boss told him he needed to work in Chicago, so we moved here. The flight from Incheon to Chicago took over twelve hours, and it was exhausting. It was not my first time on a plane, but it was my first long-haul flight.

When I arrived, I was so nervous because everyone spoke English. I worried that if I made a mistake, I would be in trouble. At immigration, people were asked questions like, "Why are you here? Do you have a visa?" I stood in line, and when it was my turn, I just kept answering, "Yes, yes, yes," even when I did not fully understand the questions.

Stepping outside the airport, I saw the cars and traffic signs and thought, "Oh, I'm really in the US." When I saw my new house for the first time, I was shocked. It was huge—at least twice the size of my old house. During my first week, I saw a yellow school bus for the first time, which amazed me because I had only seen them in movies and cartoons. It felt surreal.

For the first month, I attended summer school at Stevenson, where I met other students for the first time. Before that, I spent most of my time in my room. I was nervous, but it was okay because there were other students from different countries who also could not speak English well. I even met other students from South Korea, which made things easier.

One of the biggest cultural differences was how people address elders. In Korea, we bow deeply, about seventy-five degrees at the waist. In the US, people just say "hi" and wave. That was new to me. Also, the way people say "bless you" after sneezing was confusing at first, since we do not do that in Korea.

Everything here is bigger—the buildings, the roads, and even the school system. There are so many clubs and sports activities at school. I had never seen a school with its own store before. The variety of foods and people was also new. Even though I had studied English in Korea, I struggled with idioms and casual expressions that I had not learned before.

At home, I developed a new hobby—playing the guitar. I took a guitar class in my freshman year and found it really fun, so I bought a guitar and started practicing. I also enjoy watching movies with my friends. At first, it was difficult to watch movies without subtitles because English sounded so fast, but now I have gotten used to it. On weekends, I spend a lot of time at home baking desserts like cookies and pound cakes. I am still not skilled enough to bake big cakes, but I am improving.

School was really difficult at first, but now I enjoy it. I have made friends in every class. My favorite subject is math because I liked it in Korea, and I also have a lot of friends in my math class.

As for the future, I do not have a specific plan yet, but I want to have a positive influence. Everyone wants to be a positive influence, but for me, I want to give hope to others who are immigrating to the US or just struggling with something new. I want to show them that if I can do it, they can too. I want to encourage people and help them feel less afraid about moving to a new country.

Visiting Chicago for the first time was amazing. The city was huge and beautiful, with so many tall buildings. My father took me and my mom to a restaurant that sold deep-dish pizza. I was excited to try it, and when I did, it was amazing—so much cheese! I love cheese. Even small details, like license plates on cars, were new to me. Each state has different designs, and some even have pictures on them. I thought that was really cool.

Overall, moving to the US has been a big change, but I am adjusting. There are challenges, but also new experiences that I never expected. I hope to keep growing and helping others who go through the same journey.

VIDEO LINKS

greencardvoices.org/speakers/daeyun-lee

EUROPE
Shostka,
Ukraine

Tymur Tatsenyuk

Born: Shostka, Ukraine

"ON THE SECOND OR THIRD DAY OF THE INVASION, I REMEMBER LOOKING OUT THE WINDOW AND SEEING A WHOLE ROW OF UKRAINIAN TANKS RIGHT UNDER OUR BUILDING."

The Ukraine invasion started on February 24, 2022. We were in Kyiv, sleeping, when my grandma called my mom at 4:00 a.m. and said that the Russians had started the war. We could not believe it, so we turned on the TV and watched the news. The whole day, we just sat there, watching and trying to get updates. On the second day, we went to a bunker—it was an underground garage in a nearby building. We were only a few kilometers from our home when a huge explosion went off. I do not know exactly what it was, but it was big. So we went back to the bunker, but the next day, I got sick because it was really cold. After that, we did not go back.

I was born in Shostka, but we moved a few years later, when I was ten or a little younger. I moved to Kyiv, and lived there for a few years before the invasion. My life was good. I was going to school, getting decent grades—probably good grades. I love math and English, and maybe biology. I spent time with my friends and family. We would go on long walks—like two hours in the parks with my mom—and we went on boat rides together. My friends and I had scooters, and we rode all over Kyiv, doing tricks and stuff. I remember once we went into an abandoned building—it was pretty scary, but we left after an hour.

My family includes my mom Vitalina, my first aunt Inna, and my second aunt Alina, as well as their husbands, Igor and Oleksandr. Inna and Igor have two children; one is Eva, and the newborn's name is Vladislav. My other aunt and uncle, Alina and Oleksandr, have one newborn named Miroslava. Also, I have my grandma Tatiana and my grandfather Sergei. He unfortunately died in 2016, but I do not really remember much from that time. My mom had a cousin named Anatolii; he unfortunately died due to Russian soldiers. I wish him the best.

On the second or third day of the invasion, I remember looking out the window and seeing a whole row of Ukrainian tanks right under our building. The whole house was shaking. After about two weeks, on my mom's birthday—March 6, 2022—she decided we had to leave Ukraine. It was not safe. Our family was in another city, and it was safe there, but we could not go because the Russians were controlling the roads. We had no choice but to go to the train station and try to leave. But unexpectedly, the Russians blew up the train route, so our train got delayed for hours on the way to Lviv.

When we got to Lviv, we were supposed to take a bus to Poland, but it was super crowded. People were pushing to buy tickets. Thankfully, I managed to squeeze through the crowd and buy tickets for me and my mom. We finally made it to Poland. It was full of Ukrainians trying to escape, but we saw a program that helped Ukrainians in Poland, so we decided to stay for a while. I do not remember exactly what city we were in, but from there, we took a train across Poland. That train ride was really tough—we stood for ten hours straight. Eventually, we traveled throughout Sweden from Stockholm to Luleå. After a few months of living there, we heard about a program that helped Ukrainians get to the US, and we saw our opportunity.

The biggest challenges I faced during this time were the train routes getting blown up by the Russians; money, because we did not have much; and the language barrier. Polish is similar to Ukrainian, but not the same, so we could not always understand people. Thankfully, a lot of them spoke English, so I could still communicate. My mom knows some Polish since it is close to Ukrainian, but still, some words were different, and people had to explain things to us.

To go to the US, we needed sponsors to sign documents. My mom recorded a video in Ukrainian and posted it on Facebook and Ukrainian forums, asking for help. She was crying a lot in the video. She explained how her brother—well, actually her cousin—was killed by the Russians. A couple of American people agreed to sponsor us. With our last bit of money, we bought plane tickets and flew to the US. We arrived in New York City, then lived in Connecticut for a few months before moving to Chicago because of the big Ukrainian community there.

Shostka is really close to the Russian border—maybe 100 kilometers or so. It is much farther from Kyiv, because Kyiv is in the middle of Ukraine, and Shostka is in Sumy Oblast, which is a pretty big distance away. I lost a lot of my friends when I left, but one of them also escaped Ukraine. He lives in Spain now.

We did not want to leave Ukraine, but we had no choice. The rest of our family stayed because their husbands were in Ukraine, so they could not leave. But thankfully, they are all alive and doing okay. We left Sweden because my mom could not find a job. Swedish is a really hard language to learn. I tried, but my tongue just could not get it right—it is hard to explain.

The difference in the US is that people speak English—thankfully, the English education in Ukraine is pretty good, so I could already understand and speak a decent amount. I learned a lot more English from movies and talking to people at school. My mom, though, did not know any English at first. Now she knows a little—simple sentences—but she still struggles to understand people. When she was in school, they did not teach English well. Her teacher focused more on German than English, even though he was supposed to be an English teacher. My mom does not remember anything from that time when her English teacher was teaching her German.

The first few weeks in the US were good. People helped us a lot and taught us about life here. I learned more English words I did not know before, because even though my English was okay, I did not understand everything. People used more complex words than I was used to, but I learned quickly. I also started learning Spanish, which I am still learning now.

We moved to Chicago because my mom saw opportunities here, and the Ukrainian community is really big, one of the biggest in the US. We rented an apartment and settled in.

At first, I went to school for about a month; then I did summer school for a whole semester. When we got to Chicago, school was about to start, but I did not go for the first few weeks because we had not found a school near us. Then we moved again, to another place within Chicago, and I started seventh grade there.

I have been in Chicago for about two years and a few months now. I like going to school, though sometimes I try harder to get good grades than other times. I am really into computer science, coding, and stuff. I am learning Python and Java in school right now, and I think these skills that I will learn at school will be useful throughout my future coding career. I play video games, and I work out regularly. I have friends, but we mostly play games together online instead of hanging out in person.

With my family, we gather for birthdays and holidays, but mostly, we just call our family in Ukraine to wish them things like "Happy Birthday,"

"Happy Thanksgiving," "Merry Christmas," and "Happy New Year." Usually, my mom calls them. I do not call much.

I hope I become really good at computer science and go to a great university to study it. Then I want to help my family and other people, maybe even through streaming. Right now, I cannot really help because I am still a kid, but I want to study hard, get good grades, and learn more about computer science so I can do something meaningful. I think I am a good person now, but I want to keep improving.

I just hope the war in Ukraine ends, and that people stay alive.

VIDEO LINKS

greencardvoices.org/speakers/tymur-tatsenyuk

SOUTH AMERICA
Venezuela

Jhovanna

Born: Venezuela **Raised:** Panama

"I WANT TO BE ONE OF THE PEOPLE WHO SAVE LIVES. I WANT TO HELP PEOPLE. THAT IS WHAT I WANT TO DO."

I was born in Venezuela, in a small town. I was seven years old when I left Venezuela. I was living well. I had a house, but my mom left Venezuela when I was five years old. I did not see her for two years; I lived with my grandparents and my brother.

When I was given the opportunity to go to Panama to reunite with my mother, I went with my grandma and my brother. We lived in Panama for six years. We had a good life, but at the same time it was bad because there was too much xenophobia. My brother was bullied.

In 2022, my mom saw that Venezuelan people were immigrating to the USA. We saw it as a chance to go. My parents' legal stay in Panama ended and we had to move, but we could not move back to Venezuela because the economic situation was really bad at that time. We stayed in Panama for one more year. In July of 2023, my mom decided to go to the USA.

We sold all of our stuff. There was trouble to come. We had days without sleep, without eating. We walked too much for hours, for days. We feared that ICE would give us back to Venezuela. We were always running away. When we arrived in Mexico, we stayed in a smaller city for one week. Then the people started running away because ICE was there, so we escaped. We stayed in La Ciudad de México for two months. We stayed with a family that welcomed us to their house. Finally, my mom said that she was not going to wait anymore for the TPS. We decided to give ourselves to ICE at the border.

We crossed a river with an inflatable mattress. When we crossed, we walked a little bit, and then people started flashing lights and saying, "Get your hands up." We started to walk a little bit more. We had to wait from 10:00 p.m. to 4:00 a.m. We were cold and went days without sleep. The bus arrived, and they got us to a refugee center. There, they had us sign immigration papers. We waited for fourteen hours. They just give us apples and water to eat. They separated me from my mom and my dad, and they also separated my brother.

My mom and my dad were separated too. We stayed like that for twelve hours. There were Honduran people there who had been waiting for weeks. I was afraid of not seeing my parents.

Then they took our things and brought them to where my parents were. They got us to another refugee center because we had no money to travel to Chicago. They got us to a refugee center where we had to wait for the bus. There were a hundred people in that refugee center. We just got to eat a little rice with beans and water, just that. When the bus got there, it took us to Chicago.

When I arrived in Chicago, they enrolled me in school. In the school, the children bullied me and my brother, more so my brother. For me, they mostly just said bad words or "Go back to your country." But for my brother, they pushed him, hit him, and insulted him. It was really hard in that school. That school just speaks English. No one speaks Spanish—no teachers, no children, nobody. My brother was alone. We could not talk to the teachers and tell them we were being bullied. When the opportunity was given, my brother said, "Oh, they are bullying me," but they did not believe him, so it just stayed like that. My brother is still in that school because my parents live so close, and we cannot move.

When I got to the school where I am now, I really started to feel more happy and more confident. Now, I can talk about my life with my friends, with people I really trust because they can talk my language. I can say what I want. I can do what my brother really cannot.

I like to play volleyball. It is closed now because it is winter. I prefer to study and do sports. In school, I do jewelry. I learned how to cook. I like to spend more time with my friends. When we hang out, we go to eat or we go to a park.

My favorite subject is history now, but before, it was English. I really like to learn new languages and new things. That is what my career is about. I would like to do anesthesiology. That is a thing that I really want to do. I want to study that. I really like to learn about us, about our bodies. I really would like to do that. In my free time, I like to watch a series of surgeries.

I want to be one of the people who save lives. I want to help people. That is what I want to do. When I was in trouble from coming here, there were too many people that did not have a doctor or anybody. If they go to the hospital, they can be deported. If they are sick, they cannot go. If they fall, they cannot go. I really want to help people. If they are in a situation where they cannot pay or something like that, I can help them. I really want to do that.

VIDEO LINKS

greencardvoices.org/speakers/jhovanna

ASIA
Durgapur,
West Bengal,
India

Nilarnab Roy

Born: Durgapur, West Bengal, India

"I AM VERY THANKFUL TO MY PARENTS FOR BRINGING ME HERE AND GIVING ME THIS OPPORTUNITY."

I came from India. My country is situated in the Asian continent on the east side, with water on the three sides: the Bay of Bengal, the Arabian Sea, and the Indian Ocean. It has great mountains like the Himalayas, which have the highest mountain peak, Mount Everest, on the north side. Because the ocean was on three sides where I lived, it was very windy. The main foods we ate in our home country were rice, pulses, and roti. The most famous food in India is biryani, which is one of my favorite foods. Our traditional clothes are dhoti kurtas for men and sarees for women.

I had many home responsibilities, like looking after my sister and helping my mother. We lived in an apartment in Kolkata in the state of West Bengal in India. I studied at Mangalam Vidya Niketan, which is a private school. I studied from elementary to grade nine. There, I had many good friends in my school. My daily routine was the same as here for weekdays. Every day was very similar—going to school, doing homework, and following a structured schedule. I like the rich culture and tradition of India, but I dislike that it is overcrowded.

I travel sometimes during winter vacation and summer vacation. Sometimes I traveled because of my father's job, or sometimes just for vacation, visiting places like Chennai and Assam. I once came to America in 2018 because of my father's job, just for one month, just to visit. He was here for three years, from 2016 to 2019, so when I came here again, I was very excited about it.

My family told me the news when I had just started grade nine in India. I was near my unit assessment, but suddenly my father told me we were moving to Chicago for a better education, a better life, and better health. I came here on the second of August, 2024.

After buying the tickets, a problem with something from my dad's office meant we had to wait a while, until the second of August. My father had been in Chicago for two months before we came. When we arrived, my dad's office gave us a rental home for thirty days; during that time, we had to find another house where we would live, and we also had to buy a car.

For the first week in Chicago, I had jet lag, but I overcame it. For the next two or three weeks, we were going shopping, and everything was new to us, so we bought many things from the shop. After I had been here a month, I started to go to school. Starting a new school was a little challenging, as I was having trouble understanding the language and speaking up. Soon, I made many friends, and they helped me when I had trouble.

My parents and I sacrificed a lot to come to the US. I had to restart everything here. We left our family like our grandparents, uncles, aunts, and cousins. It was a big challenge for us. In my previous school, I had many friends, but one, Sashwata, was my best friend—I still remember him.

I currently live in Vernon Hills, Illinois. I live with my parents and my younger sister. I am currently studying at Stevenson High School, where I am learning more new things and skills. I have made many friends who help when I am in trouble, as I am new here and learning new things. My hobbies are painting, playing violin, and taking photographs. I knew about all this before, but after coming here, I am learning more. I am having a healthy life and getting a better education. I think I am the same person, but in a different part of the world. Everything seemed new to me at first, but now I am used to it.

I am very thankful to my parents for bringing me here and giving me this opportunity. I will contribute to this country by helping others and doing good things. I am thinking of working on technological advancements here. I will learn about engineering and all the things related to my hobbies. In this school, there are many clubs and activities for these things, so I will be doing them.

VIDEO LINKS

greencardvoices.org/speakers/nilarnab-roy

ASIA
Chirchik,
Uzbekistan

Dariya Zhevakina

Born: Chirchik, Uzbekistan **Raised:** Kaliningrad, Russia

"I NEVER THOUGHT I WOULD BECOME A MODEL, JUST LIKE I NEVER THOUGHT I WOULD LEAVE MY HOME IN UZBEKISTAN. BUT LIFE HAS A WAY OF REWRITING OUR STORIES."

I was born in Uzbekistan on December 20, 2006, in a city called Chirchiq. I lived there until I was nine years old before moving to Russia. My childhood in Uzbekistan was amazing. I am really happy I had that childhood because it was full of joy and fun. I did not go to kindergarten, since I had a big family—lots of aunts, uncles, grandparents—so I spent most of my time with my siblings. It was always fun being with my brothers and sisters.

After that, I moved to Russia, to a city called Kaliningrad, which is on the Baltic Sea. It is a really beautiful place. That was when I started living a more mature life. I found really good friends and began my teenage years there. It was a great time, but I always missed Uzbekistan—its food, culture, and atmosphere. I often thought about traveling back. However, we moved to Russia for a better education, and those six years in Kaliningrad were really good.

In Kaliningrad, I lived with my immediate family—my father, mother, and younger brothers. In Uzbekistan, though, we had a much larger family, with grandparents, aunts, uncles, and my other siblings—three more sisters and two more brothers. Life in Kaliningrad was different, but I enjoyed spending time with my family and making new friends.

One summer evening, I had just come home from a walk with friends when my mom told me, "Dasha, at the end of October 2022, we're moving to the US." I was shocked. I had already planned to go to college in Kaliningrad and had set my goals for the future. I kept asking, "Why?" but my mom just said she would tell me later. All I knew was that we were leaving at the end of October.

We began our journey from Kaliningrad, but before moving to the US, we traveled to Uzbekistan to spend time with our extended family. No one knew that we had sold everything in Russia and that we were not coming back. When my parents finally told my grandparents, my grandmother cried. She was heartbroken that we were moving so far away.

From Uzbekistan, we traveled to Turkey and then to Mexico. At first, it felt like just a family trip. We spent time in Cancun for two weeks, enjoying the sun and the ocean. I was only fifteen, and I didn't fully understand the difficulty of what my parents were going through. It was just another trip for me. But when we arrived in Tijuana, I started to realize the seriousness of our situation. That was when reality hit.

Crossing the border into the US was incredibly difficult. I was sick in Tijuana, and it was hard to stay calm. I kept thinking about my friends in Kaliningrad, knowing I would not see them again anytime soon. I cried every night. We attempted to cross multiple times, but the border police kept sending us back to our hotel. At one point, while trying to cross, a man pulled a gun on us and told us to leave. My parents were close to giving up. It felt like a nightmare.

We had nothing left—no home, no belongings, just our family and some savings from selling everything in Russia. My parents knew we had no choice but to keep trying. Finally, at 4:00 a.m., while I was half asleep in the car, I heard my parents whispering. We had made it across the border on our fourth try.

When we arrived, I could not believe we were actually in the US. My friends back home started checking my location, realizing I was now on the other side of the world. It was both overwhelming and exciting. I knew I had to start over—find a new school, make new friends, and plan for a new future. It was difficult, but at the same time, it felt like a dream.

Adjusting to life in the US was not easy. I had never thought I would need English. Back in seventh grade in Russia, I even told my mom, "Why do I have to learn English? It's too hard." But now, I had no choice. For the first few months, I could not communicate, and it was frustrating. But eventually, I started speaking, and to my surprise, I picked it up quickly. I never imagined I would be able to speak English confidently, but now I do.

Everything was different—houses, people, culture, even small things like toilet paper and grocery stores. I started a Telegram blog to show my life in the US, and my followers from Russia and Uzbekistan were fascinated by the differences. They kept asking, "What's this? What's that like?" It made me realize how little people knew about life here.

School was a challenge at first. I thought it would be easier because I am a very social person, but American students were different than those in Russia. They had different interests, hobbies, and ways of interacting. Still, I made friends by being open and curious. They were interested in my background, asking about my life in Russia and how I ended up in the US. Over time, I formed strong friendships and learned to navigate this new world.

Life is good now. We are much better off than when we first arrived. I live with my parents and younger brothers in a house, and we celebrate holidays together. Our second Thanksgiving here was especially memorable—we decorated our home beautifully and truly enjoyed the moment. Looking back at our first year compared to now, I can see how much we have adjusted and grown.

I am currently working as a model. I travel for photo and video shoots, not just in Chicago but in different states. I also have a passion for creative work, like photography and designing decorations. I never thought I would become a model, just like I never thought I would leave my home in Uzbekistan. But life has a way of rewriting our stories. Besides that, I love diving, surfing, and other hobbies that keep me active.

In the future, I hope that I will be a really good model. I am deciding which college I want to attend. Because I'm from Russia, I think it can help me in the future. I can communicate in different languages, and I will continue learning English more, which it will help my modeling career. I have found my job that I want to do, that I am interested in, and I want to keep doing this.

VIDEO LINKS

greencardvoices.org/speakers/dariya-zhevakina

MÉXICO
SOUTH AMERICA
Mexico

Joselyn

Born: Mexico

"IN THE FUTURE, I JUST WANT TO STUDY AND HAVE A JOB. I DO NOT KNOW WHAT I AM GOING TO STUDY YET, BUT I WANT TO HAVE A JOB SO I HAVE AN INCOME AND GET TO CONTRIBUTE TO SOCIETY."

I was born in Cuernavaca, Morelos, in Mexico. When I was a child, I would go outside with my cousin and my brother. I lived in a small town, literally small. We did not have parks or anything like that; we just played around.

I moved to Guerrero when I was eight years old. When I was that age, my dad died. It was difficult for me, my mom, and my older brother. I started school there, and I finished middle school.

When I was ten years old, my mom married my stepdad. My stepdad is a US citizen living in Chicago. Then, in 2022, we moved to Chicago to start our life together. My brother had to stay behind, because he was twenty-four years old at the time. He is married with kids. I am a tía to one boy; he is two years old now.

We had to give our things up. We went to Ciudad Juárez to get our papers, then to El Paso, Texas, to fly in the plane to Chicago. When I arrived to Chicago, I was nervous but also excited because I did not know this place. It was something new. My first week was weird because I did not know anything here. And it was so cold—like, really cold. I noticed everything was different, even my clothes. I saw things I had never seen before such as tall buildings, restaurants, and people from different backgrounds. It was weird because I did not speak English. I could not talk with them. It was really difficult.

One of the hard things in Chicago is, I miss my brother. I miss my family back at home. When I started seventh grade after I came here, it was difficult because I did not speak English. The kids gave me weird looks because of that. It was bad for me. It felt like a new world for me.

Right now, I live in an apartment in the Little Village neighborhood. Life now is good. I have friends. I can talk with my cousins in Mexico using Snapchat. I am able to visit Mexico. I attend high school. I feel comfortable with the people around me. I feel happy now. I got back two days ago from traveling to Mexico for a week, and it was the most beautiful thing, because I did not go a year ago. It was so fun. I got to see my friends and my brother. I got to dance at Jaripeos.

We have also visited Indiana several times because I have some family there—cousins and my aunt, my mom's sister. It is good there. I play flag football, and I like to go outside with my friends. We go to the stores shopping for clothes with my mom. I like it.

My favorite subject is science. In the future, I just want to study and have a job. I do not know what I am going to study yet, but I want to have a job so I have an income and get to contribute to society.

VIDEO LINKS

greencardvoices.org/speakers/joselyn

ASIA
Bishkek,
Kyrgyzstan

Aruuke Moldalieva

Born: Bishkek, Kyrgyzstan

"PEOPLE THINK WHEN YOU MOVE HERE FROM ANOTHER COUNTRY THAT YOU HAVE TWO CULTURES, BUT ACTUALLY YOU HAVE NONE."

I was born in Kyrgyzstan, in the capital city of Bishkek, in 2008. I first attended elementary school there at a Turkish private school. Later, I transferred to a public school, where I focused on math and computer science.

I have three younger sisters, and we grew up with our mom and dad. We lived in Bishkek for a year or two when I was very young before moving to another city, Osh, in the south of Kyrgyzstan. That is where my younger sister was born. My parents traveled to Turkey often, sometimes for work and sometimes for holidays. Sometimes, my siblings and I went with them. Then, after several years in Osh, we moved back to Bishkek for my parents' work.

My mom always dreamed of sending me to college in the United States. Osh was a very small place, and people did not think of living any farther away than Bishkek. They thought the idea of living in the United States was a joke. My mom is the person who dreams a lot and who taught me to dream. My family was planning to have me apply for an exchange program in the United States, but then we got our green card. For about four or five years, we had applied for the US green card lottery. Every year, we would take family pictures against a white background for the application. We never really believed we would win—it was just something we did, almost for fun. Then, one day in May 2023, we opened our email and saw that my mom had won the green card lottery. At first, my parents were confused, trying to understand if it was real. But somehow, I knew immediately. Even though I did not speak English, I understood what it meant. I remember my mom screaming and jumping with excitement while my dad and I stared at the computer, still in shock. That moment was unforgettable.

After that, we began preparing our documents and medical exams. At first, we planned to move to Texas, not Illinois. We were so close to settling in Texas, but our plans changed. One of the hardest parts of leaving was selling some of our belongings. We packed twelve suitcases, and I remember my dad injuring his arm while handling them at the airport. Despite all that, we still left a lot of things behind in Kyrgyzstan.

Before we left, we had many visitors. In our culture, hosting and visiting guests is very important, and our house was filled with family and friends saying goodbye. I also had a small farewell party with four of my closest friends. I got them personalized T-shirts with memories and inside jokes as a parting gift. Today, I am still in touch with two of them.

Looking back, I realize I gave up everything I had known. I lost many friends, a part of my culture, and even my language. Since I do not speak my first language often here, I feel like I am slowly losing that connection.

Our journey to the US started at the airport in Kyrgyzstan. We flew to Turkey first because there were no direct flights. It was a six-hour flight, followed by a six-hour layover in Istanbul. Then, we boarded another plane to Chicago. In total, the trip took twenty-seven hours. When we landed in Chicago, I felt completely lost. My family did too. The only one who spoke English was my dad, and even he struggled. I remember how difficult it was just to find our suitcases at the airport.

We had some family in Chicago—cousins, an uncle, and an aunt. My cousin also lives here and visits us often. We also have relatives in other states, like Pennsylvania. One of our Chicago relatives picked us up and drove us to the house we had rented for a week. At first, we did not have a car, so we walked everywhere—even to Walmart, which was far and exhausting. The only food we had brought from Kyrgyzstan was small packets of instant noodles. That was our first week.

We arrived in April, and my sister and I enrolled in middle school. But since the school year was almost over, we only attended for about two weeks. I did not go to the graduation ceremony because I did not feel like I was really part of the school. I only had two Kyrgyz friends and one Ukrainian friend; we are still good friends today at Stevenson.

I remember my first day of middle school. In Kyrgyzstan, we wore uniforms in public schools—classic dark bottoms and white tops—so I showed up in a black skirt and a white long-sleeve shirt. Everyone stared at me because I looked different; I remember thinking they looked different too, dressed in colorful and casual clothes. That day, I also struggled with my locker—I just could not figure out how to open it.

A year later, I started high school at Stevenson. The first thing I joined was the fall cheerleading season. I continued with winter cheer and am still part of the team now. I love my team, my coaches, and the sport itself—it's something completely new to me because cheerleading is not common in Kyrgyzstan. I also love computer science. I have been programming since fourth grade, and I appreciate the higher quality of education in computer science here compared to back home.

Right now, my dad has moved back to Kyrgyzstan for work, so I live with my mom and three siblings. In my free time, I study a lot, practice cheer, and hang out with my friends. As for the future, my biggest hope is to get into my dream college. After graduating, I plan to stay in the US to work and build my life here.

I really want to share about my culture and country. I want to be part of a community and feel like I belong. People think when you move here from another country that you have two cultures, but actually you have none. Americans think of you as Kyrgyz, but people from Kyrgyzstan think of you as American.

VIDEO LINKS

greencardvoices.org/speakers/aruuke-moldalieva

EUROPE
Moscow,
Russia

Denis Dubovoi

Born: Moscow, Russia

"WHEN I ARRIVED IN THE US, IT WAS NOT MY FIRST TIME HERE, BUT IT WAS MY FIRST TIME AS A CITIZEN, AND I SAW THINGS DIFFERENTLY."

I was born right in the center of Moscow, and I had a usual life as a student and citizen of Russia. My days were filled with school, sports, and homework. One thing I loved about Russia was the freedom to walk everywhere without needing a car. In my free time, I enjoyed exploring the city, and my family often traveled throughout the country. We visited different attractions, parks, and restaurants.

I had been to America before I moved here. I was here seven times because my parents like to travel—we would often have a holiday or flight to Europe or somewhere else with better weather than Russia. Russia is usually cold for nine months of the year; it is not sunny, and sometimes the weather is not really good.

I have two brothers and a sister—one younger brother, a younger sister, and an older brother. We never had pets because my parents found it too difficult, especially with all the travel involved in moving to America.

When my parents won the green card lottery, I already had an idea that we might move to the US. Since my older brother had already been living in the US before we got the green card, it was not a sudden announcement from my parents—it was something I saw coming. It was only a matter of time.

My brother had been playing basketball for one of the best junior teams in Moscow. A coach he met had told my parents about a special basketball school in the US that offered great opportunities. My parents thought it would be good for him—he could improve his basketball skills, learn English, and get a quality education. That is how my brother ended up moving to America first.

The hardest part of moving to the US was the journey itself. Traveling from Russia is expensive and time-consuming—it took us around four days. For my younger sister, who was only five years old at the time, it was especially tough. Ten hours on a plane, ten hours on a train—it was exhausting for her. That was one of the most challenging aspects of the trip.

Due to the war, we had to leave Russia through Europe first, which was complicated. Getting a visa was difficult; three different countries declined our applications. Since American embassies no longer operate in Russia, we had to go through extra steps to get our visas. Additionally, there were medical procedures—X-rays, health checkups, and even an examination of a surgery my hand had undergone to confirm that my parents had not harmed me. It took my parents nearly half a year to collect all the necessary documents.

When I came here in 2023, my parents chose Chicago as our destination because it has good flight connections to Russia, and it is a major city with many opportunities. There are also good colleges and schools—it is one of the best cities for education in the entire country, which was important to my family. Additionally, Chicago makes it easier to obtain visas for European countries such as Spain, where we could potentially get citizenship.

We still have many things left in Russia, including our apartment, but the trip itself was an adventure. First, we had to take a ten-hour train ride to another city, then drive for five hours to a European country. From there, we flew to another part of Europe, which was a five-hour flight; finally, we took a ten-hour flight to the US. Every time I travel back to Russia, it takes even longer, sometimes with an extra fifteen or twenty hours stuck at the border. It is a long and exhausting process.

When I arrived in the US, it was not my first time here, but it was my first time as a citizen, and I saw things differently. I had to adjust to new ways of thinking and living. One of the biggest challenges was realizing how essential a car is in America. In Russia, I spent my free time walking around with friends, but here, the only place I can walk to is a gas station.

Language was another major hurdle. At school, I struggled to understand and speak English. After five hours of classes, I felt like someone had hit me on the head with a hammer. It was overwhelming. In biology class, for example, I barely understood anything because of the slang and advanced vocabulary I had not learned in Russia. The first week of school was especially tough.

Now, life in the US is better. I have many friends, all of whom speak Russian, which makes things easier. My main hobby here is playing squash. There are not as many squash players here as there are in Russia, but it is a great way to make new friends.

On holidays, I usually spend time with friends. We walk around the forest or hang out at the gas station—our usual spot. Otherwise, life as a student in America is mostly about studying, hanging out with friends, and playing computer games.

My dream is to go to college here, preferably in Chicago because I want to stay closer to my family. As for returning to Russia, it depends on how things in the world change. I spent more than half my life in Russia, and even if I live in America for another ten years, I think I will still want to go back at some point.

VIDEO LINKS

greencardvoices.org/speakers/denis-dubovoi

ASIA
Almaty,
Kazakhstan

Anastassiya Nartova

Born: Almaty, Kazakhstan

"I DO NOT KNOW WHO I AM GOING TO BE IN THE FUTURE, BUT I REALLY WANT TO FIND MYSELF, TO FIND WHAT I LIKE AND DO NOT LIKE."

I am from Kazakhstan, specifically Almaty. Almaty is almost the capital, but not quite. It is a city where many people speak Russian, as I do. When I think of my home country, I am reminded of my friends, my family, and my closest relatives. My life in Kazakhstan revolved around five things: family, sports, school, friends, and pets.

We always lived in our own house—in a home with a backyard and a big garden filled with trees. My family built the house, which took two years to complete. In the summer, we had to water the trees regularly. It was a beautiful green space that I miss dearly. In the yard, we had two large dogs, Oscar and Christa. They lived outside our home, but they were part of our family for many years. We also had a parrot named Prince, whom we got when I was in first grade. He was tiny and yellow, and he chose me as his person. In the second grade, we got a small dog named Sam. Over the years, we also had fish, a frog, chickens, ducks, rabbits, and other pets.

Like any other kid, I attended a regular school and made friends. In fourth grade, my parents encouraged me and my younger brother to start sports. I took up swimming, and after three years, I joined a sports school. Swimming became my life. I trained morning and evening, went to school in between, and barely had time for anything else. Over time, I reached a high level, earning a Candidate in Master of Sports title in swimming. The sports team became my second family. I competed in many tournaments and had incredible experiences. However, by the end of eighth grade, I developed back pain because of the trauma and the intense training. Around the same time, I learned that we would move from Kazakhstan.

My mother had always dreamed of living near the ocean, but Kazakhstan does not have any. The education system was also getting worse each year, and inflation made life unpredictable. My parents wanted a better future for me and my brother, so they decided to move. Initially, we considered Canada, and there was even a plan for me and my father to move there first while my mother and brother followed two years later. But it was complicated, and the family would struggle with the separation. Eventually, my parents applied for visas to the US and were approved. We saw this as an opportunity.

We did not choose Chicago from the start. First, my parents traveled to New York while my brother and I stayed with our grandmother in Almaty. Our parents spent time there and weighed the pros and cons before deciding there were more pros—it was the best option for our future.

When they returned, they began selling our belongings, including our house. Finding new homes for our pets was one of the hardest parts. I had to say goodbye to my parrot Prince and our big dogs, but we managed to bring Sam with us. Getting his travel documents was complicated because pets do not often fly from Kazakhstan.

Leaving was emotional. The hardest moment was saying goodbye to my cousin, who was like a sister to me. At the airport, we hugged for the last time, knowing we would not see each other again for a long time. The journey to the US was long—a six-hour flight, a ten-hour layover, and another fourteen-hour flight. We were most worried about Sam—all this time he was alone, and we did not know where he was.

When we arrived in New York in the summer of 2023, the immigration officer at passport control initially said we could not enter. My mother, who spoke the best English in our family, managed to explain—after a tense moment, he finally said, "Welcome to the US." We could not find our dog at first, but when we finally got him, he was so happy.

The first thing I remember about New York was the subway—the speed of the trains, the loud whooshing sound they made when they slowed down, and the American flags everywhere. It felt surreal. We stayed in a hotel at first. The time difference made everything feel strange. The first few days were a blur, adjusting to a new country, a new language, and a new life.

For three months, we lived in New York in a tiny space—just two rooms and a bathroom, much smaller than our house in Kazakhstan. It was overwhelming. I cried a lot, missing my parrot, my cousin, and my old life. My parents were constantly busy with paperwork, while my brother and I, who had no internet and little to do, stayed at that place where we lived. But we walked around the city, played basketball, and tried to adjust.

My parents eventually decided New York was not the right place for us—too many crowds, too much movement, and too much crime. They had friends in Chicago, also from Almaty, so we moved there.

Chicago was quieter and greener. We found a bigger place to live, and in September of 2023, my brother and I started school. He went to middle school, and I went to high school. Despite having already changed schools multiple times because of the sports in Kazakhstan, I was terrified. Everything was different—the people, the language, the system. I was so scared to go to school that it came down to denial—I did not want to go to school, I was scared of the unknown. On my first day, I had a transfer buddy to guide me to my first class, but after that, I was on my own. Over time, I found friends and adjusted.

School in the US was different, especially math. In Kazakhstan, teachers did not always teach properly, and I struggled with it. Here, math was structured differently, and I started at an easier level. Within a year, I moved up to a harder level and was getting A's. I also loved art—drawing and painting.

I had thought I would never return to swimming after leaving Kazakhstan, but here, sports were a big part of student life. I wanted to join the swim team, but the season had already started, so I joined water polo instead. It was completely different from swimming but still in the water. It also forced me to speak English, since my teammates did not speak Russian. Later, I joined the swim team, but after a two-year break, I could not perform at my previous level. Still, I enjoyed it, and I might join both sports again.

I keep in touch with my cousin through video calls, and my father often calls my grandmother. Right now, we may need to get another kind of visa. It's kind of complicated, and my parents work a lot because they need to get more money. They understand that if my brother and I can be educated here in colleges and universities, we are going to be able to work in really good professions.

I do not know who I am going to be in the future, but I really want to find myself, to find what I like and do not like, to find more people, because I like to be friends with everybody. My friends tell me that I am so kind, but I don't know—I think I am. For the future, my goal is to focus on my education, improve my English, and gain more experience. I also want to visit Kazakhstan again one day—to see my family, my friends, and the places I grew up. But seeing my parrot again would be too emotional. I am not sure how he would react, and it scares me.

Four of us arrived in the US with just two suitcases, leaving behind everything we had ever known. At first, I missed even the smallest things, like my colored pencils. It made me realize how much we take for granted. But despite all the challenges, I know this journey was worth it. I am proud of my parents for making this difficult decision, and I am hopeful for what the future holds.

VIDEO LINKS

greencardvoices.org/speakers/anastassiya-nartova

AFRICA
Accra,
Ghana

Josephine Akpai

Born: Accra, Ghana

"AT SOME POINT, EVERYBODY IS GOING TO NEED HELP—WHY NOT HELP OTHERS?"

Growing up in Ghana as a young girl was very fun. I enjoyed it very much, from playing with my friends on the street to visiting my neighbor's house. It was a very fun experience going to a private school where there were strict rules, then having to go back home where nobody really cared what you did, saw, or looked like. Everything was just very flexible for me, and I enjoyed it very much. Coming to the US was kind of a surprise to me, and assimilating to new environments and new people was very difficult and confusing to me. Growing up in Ghana, to me, was easier than growing up here.

When I was around seven years old, one day my Mom started packing. When I asked her, "Oh, where are we going?" she said, "Oh, we're going to your dad's house." A week later, I got in the car with my dad and mom, and we drove to the airport. I did not think about it that much, since I was a child. I thought we were just going to my dad's house, or a hotel or something. We got to the airport, and I sat at the terminal; then I saw planes, and I asked my mom, "What's that?" She said, "Oh, that's an airplane."

Two days later, after boarding the plane, we arrived in Chicago in late 2017. It was a bit confusing, but I was very happy that my aunt was here to guide us and give us shelter and comfort us through it all.

To be here in the US, I really gave up a lot of stuff, like moving away from my father, my friends, and other people who cared about me dearly. I lost contact with my sister, although we are not related—she is somebody I grew up with, and I have always called her my sister. Giving up all of that overwhelmed me as a child. I am glad that I found a new community of people to depend on and learn from.

When I landed in Chicago, I remember my aunt handing me a coat and taking me and my mom to go get Garrett's popcorn.

It took me about a week to get enrolled into school. Honestly, I was kind of annoyed, because as a child I did not like going out much. While we were going through the enrollment process, I thought we were doing some other stuff that had nothing to do with me; then, one week later, I was in school with new people. On my first day of school, everybody was looking at me weird; it was quite embarrassing, because I did not know if they were judging me or intrigued. I feel as if many people thought that I knew nothing, but I could understand them very well. I grew up speaking English. I would hear people say things about me, and in my head, I was like, I know what you're saying. So it was kind of embarrassing.

In Ghana, I would not say I lived in a horrible place. I lived in a middle-class home. I had my own bedroom, a fully furnished house with everything. It was a very amazing place to me, and leaving there hurt me. Everyday life was going to school, coming back home, taking a shower, and then maybe going to play with the neighborhood kids, or doing your homework and then eating.

In Ghana, there were not many grocery stores next to me. The stores that we had were local markets. Sometimes I would go shopping at the flea markets with my mom. We would also go to boutiques when we went to where my dad lived.

My dad is a firefighter and lives in Ada by the coast of Ghana. My mom takes care of me because of his job being far away. In Ghana, my dad would frequently visit at the end of each week; when he did, he would usually take us to a resort near the beach.

I did notice a whole different side of English coming here. I knew a bunch of words people were saying, but sometimes I was like, what does that mean? And my friends would have to tell me exactly what it meant. It was a great experience learning, because I love to learn. If I did not know it, I felt uncomfortable, and I was glad that I found a way to figure out how the English that I grew up with differs from the English in America.

One obstacle I have faced is judgment from people based solely on the fact that I am an immigrant. Some people think I am here because I was seeking asylum or I was escaping from war, but I am simply here because my parents wanted a better future for me, and we had the resources to pursue it.

An opportunity here in the US is that I am very happy to experience meeting new people. I love getting to listen and hear about the differences and similarities between my culture and other cultures, and just being able to talk to other people who are different from me. But in America's eyes, we are categorized as the same people.

Right now, I live with my mom; although we may get into arguments, we enjoy each other's company very well. Some activities we participate in are cooking with each other, going grocery shopping, and going clothes shopping. During the weekdays, I go to school, and sometimes after school, I might hang out with my friends. Some weekends I spend at home, just watching TV and doing things that teenagers do. Other times, I hang out with my friends and go to new places. Sometimes on random days, my mom will take me to my auntie's house, and on special occasions she will ride us around. Those moments are the moments I enjoy the most.

As a teenager right now, I really enjoy listening to music. Music is like my second home. If I am not listening to music after school, I am attending clubs like Black Student Union and Student Voice Council, or I just have driver's education. Black Student Union is a club for students of all kinds to learn about Black culture and unite. In Student Voice Council, we organize pep rallies, events, and assemblies, we are kind of the representatives of the school. I love helping people and hearing them out. I love just learning things about people and being able to apply those skills to other things.

I am pretty sure I am going to visit Ghana either this summer or next summer. I am really looking forward to it, because I have not seen my dad in a while, and I feel like we are not that close, which kind of makes me sad.

In the future, all I know is I want to do something that helps people. I want to help the less fortunate because at some point, everybody is going to need help—why not help others? I just want to be a very helpful person in society, because in a society like this, there are many people with backgrounds like mine, and not many think they can make a difference. I want to be somebody who can make a difference.

VIDEO LINKS

greencardvoices.org/speakers/josephine-akpai

SOUTH AMERICA
Mexico

Alondra

Born: Mexico

"WHATEVER HAPPENS, I WANT TO BE A GOOD CITIZEN AND MAKE MY PARENTS PROUD."

I was born in Mexico. My home was in the countryside, and I grew up surrounded by nature. I love to explore new places and walk, and these are my favorite things. In Mexico, I lived with my family, my dad, my mom, my little sisters, and sometimes with my grandma. I miss those days in my homeland.

In Mexico, I went to secondary school [middle school]; at that time, I was so happy. I remember waking up to the beautiful views of my country; I remember times with my friends and my teachers. They were so good to me.

I moved to the US when I was fifteen years old. My dad was working several jobs. He was working as a taxi driver, a farmer, and a contractor with the municipal government. We had problems with safety, economic problems, and all that comes with being an immigrant in the United States. My dad immigrated first by himself; then my mom, my two sisters, and I immigrated afterward. It was so difficult because my sisters were so little. My little sister was seven years old; she thought we were just going to travel and return back home, but it is our hope to stay here and seek a better future for ourselves. My mom is so brave; she has sacrificed so much for us. I admire her.

When I arrived in the US, I was so nervous because I did not know where I was or where I was going. After a day or two, we took a bus to Chicago, but we stayed one day in Texas. When I say this country is different, it is because for me the houses are different, the food is different, and even the bathrooms are different. I will say this is an amazing place.

We crossed the border through CBP One. My mom said it was safer for us, but it was difficult, because we were at the border for one month waiting for the immigration appointment to cross to the US. It is okay now. My mom took care of us. She kept us safe.

When I arrived in Chicago, I felt so small because all the things are so much bigger. I saw the streets and thought it was like in the movies, because I had watched movies about Chicago. It felt like a dream, unbelievable.

When I arrived here, I arrived with my cousins and my aunts. The first months were so difficult. When I started school, I did not speak the language. I did not understand the rules or how things worked. In Mexico, for lunchtime, we can go to other places and other classrooms. But here, I went to the classroom, and security stopped me, saying, "No, no, you come back. What is in your backpack?" I went with them but did not know the language, so I just said, "Oh, okay." At that moment, I think I did not understand what they were saying, and it was so difficult.

The first day of classes in the US, I was excited; I imagined a school like those that appeared on the Disney Channel. In reality, I tried to do my best—I wanted to make many friends just like in Mexico—but the first week passed and was very difficult for me. I had not been able to make any friends; no one approached me, I had to learn to be alone and be more observant, something that I have never liked but I now know that it is necessary.

Now I am seventeen years old, in eleventh grade. I have teachers here; I love to go to parks and be part of the community, and go to school with my friends. At first, it was so difficult making friends, but with time, I made good friends, and I love it. We are exploring the city now, because I love exploring. Sometimes I go to church with my father.

For my future, I do not know what will happen, because it is difficult nowadays for immigrants. I do not know if I can just stay here, or if I will have to go; I do not know what will happen to me, and only time will tell. I do not know if I can get scholarships, but I will do my best.

I hope to be happy. Happiness for me is to be with my family—that is everything. I strive to be a good person. I want to have a career, but I know that will be difficult for me. My parents pay for everything. I want to learn everything I can to be able to help my family.

I want to learn the language better, learn from my teachers, and learn how I can stay here. I am a person who is indecisive because I do not know where I will be tomorrow. I do not know exactly what career I will choose. I want to be a pilot or a doctor, but they are too expensive. I have several options in mind, but whatever happens, I want to be a good citizen and make my parents proud.

VIDEO LINKS

greencardvoices.org/speakers/alondra

ASIA
Ulaanbaatar,
Mongolia

Budgerel (Buka) Amarsanaa

Born: Ulaanbaatar, Mongolia

"NOW, AS I BUILD MY LIFE HERE, I LOOK FORWARD TO NEW EXPERIENCES, NEW FRIENDSHIPS, AND FINDING WAYS TO CONTRIBUTE TO MY NEW COMMUNITY."

I lived in Mongolia for fifteen years before coming to the US. Mongolia is located between Russia and China. It is a big country, almost twice as big as Texas, and has only 3.4 million people. I lived with my two sisters and parents. Life in Mongolia is completely different from here—the education, transportation, language, and even social life. Everything in the US felt new and unfamiliar at first. But what I love about being here is meeting people from all over the world; it is such a great experience.

In Mongolia, traffic is a big issue, so students often walk or bike. But here, walking is not as common because there are not many pedestrian roads—you have to drive everywhere. That was a huge culture shock for me. I used to live in the capital, Ulaanbaatar, where nearly two million people reside. It is a small city compared to the US, but everything was close—markets, coffee shops, and schools were within walking distance. I miss that convenience.

The education system is also very different. In Mongolia, we had around twenty subjects per week, with different schedules every day. Here, every single day follows the same schedule for an entire semester. When I first arrived, I could not believe it. I thought, "How do students not get bored?"

The idea of moving to the US started when my mom returned from a work trip. She was amazed by the life here and all the opportunities, especially in education. She began exploring whether she could continue her education in the US; if that were to happen, our family would move with her. At first, I thought it was impossible. For us, it was just an idea. By June, when I was finishing my freshman year, I started to wonder, "What if this is my last time with my friends?" I did not take it too seriously, but by August, we had our visa appointment, and then we got approved. That was when it became real.

Telling my friends and teachers was difficult. We had a farewell party, and even though I was excited about a new experience, I did not want to leave my friends and the familiar life I had. I even told my family, "I'm not going. You can go without me." But by October 2023, we were on a plane to Chicago, where my uncle had been living for twenty years.

Our journey started in Mongolia; then we had a layover in Turkey before flying to Chicago. Looking out of the airplane window, I was shocked to see how green everything was—so many trees! When we landed, everything felt surreal. I saw so many different people, and it felt like I was in the wrong place. It was overwhelming.

At the airport, my uncle was waiting for us. I had not seen him since I was a child, so it felt strange but heartwarming to reunite. My dad and uncle hugged, and I could see their strong bond.

The first week was filled with exploration—going to stores, discovering new things, and being amazed by everything. "Look at this! Look at that!" we kept saying to each other. But before I could start school, I had to get a lot of vaccinations. Even though I had received many in Mongolia, I had to get them again as a requirement for school.

Before my first day, I met my counselor, who gave me my schedule and a tour of the school. The school was huge, much bigger than what I was used to. Another shock was that every student was given an iPad. In Mongolia, we carried heavy books for each subject, at least twenty different textbooks. Here, everything was digital, which was a big adjustment.

A Mongolian student was assigned as my transfer buddy. She showed me around and helped me feel more comfortable. I was relieved to have someone who understood what I was going through. On my first day, she even walked me to my first class. I was introduced to other Mongolian students, and they immediately welcomed me. They asked about my lunch schedule so we could eat together. Thanks to them, my first day was not as bad as I had expected.

One of the hardest things was missing my friends. I had been so close to them, and suddenly, I had no one. That loneliness made me isolate myself at first, creating a barrier that kept me from making new friends. The first six months were tough. Eventually, I accepted that I was struggling, and over time, I overcame feeling alone.

When I arrived in the middle of the school year, things were easier because I was a transfer student. But this year, I decided to fully embrace my new life. I joined clubs, made friends, and got involved. Last year, I was too shy to do anything after school, but now I stay busy with activities I love.

I joined the animal welfare club because I love animals and want to help them. A friend and I also joined the chemistry club, where we do fun experiments. One of the clubs I am most excited about is the guitar club. Now, I am finally pursuing hobbies and trying new things.

On holidays, we visit my uncle or my mom's friends and celebrate with other Mongolians. Being around people who share our traditions makes the time feel more meaningful and special.

We have also explored downtown Chicago multiple times. Each visit is different—we go to museums, try new foods, and experience new things. Food here is okay, but it is not as healthy as what we had in Mongolia. We mostly eat homemade food, but once a month, when my mom is too tired to cook, we eat out.

I have realized that I love science, but I am more interested in human-related fields than IT, which I studied in Mongolia. Whatever I choose to do in the future, I want it to be something that helps people.

Before coming here, when I got my visa, everything became real. I started noticing the smallest details—the stairs I walked on, the playground sounds, the streets, and even the way people talked. Everything suddenly felt precious. It made me think a lot about life, change, and appreciation. Knowing I had just one month left, I told myself, "Let's make it memorable." I tried new things, spent more time with friends, and made every moment count.

Now, as I build my life here, I look forward to new experiences, new friendships, and finding ways to contribute to my new community.

VIDEO LINKS

greencardvoices.org/speakers/budgerel-amarsanaa

PUMA
EUROPE
Rome,
Italy

Matvíy Buyarskyy

Born: Rome, Italy **Raised:** Ternopil, Ukraine

"SEEING AMERICA FOR THE FIRST TIME FELT LIKE A DREAM."

I was born in Rome on May 8, 2008, during the time my parents lived in Italy. They moved there since the economic situation in Ukraine was bad at the time and they were looking for work to help their growing family. When I was two years old, we moved back to Ukraine permanently. I lived in Ukraine for thirteen years. I spent most of my time in the city of Ternopil, where I studied, but I also spent time in a village called Mshanets.

My village was not big, not like other regions in Ukraine, but it was something special. It had only one main street that connected the towns, and the houses were not that big. We actually had two houses, separate from each other. If you wanted to go to the kitchen, you had to go down the stairs outside and then enter it. In the village, I had a lot of family around—grandparents, uncles, and other relatives. My grandpa was the only one living in the village home full-time because we mostly stayed in the city. It was hard for him to manage everything on his own, so every weekend we traveled to help him with his work. We also had some fields where we grew vegetables, and we kept a few animals, but not many.

Life in the village was simpler than in the city, but it was more physical. My daily routine was mostly helping my parents with anything they asked for—simple tasks like handing them things or carrying light buckets. In my free time, I spent a lot of time with my friends, though it was hard to find many because the village was really small. Still, I was lucky to find a few.

I have one younger brother, and he was one of the reasons I enjoyed my time in the village. We often rode bikes into the mountains and had fun together. One of our neighbors had a daughter, and we spent a lot of time with her too. We would go to different stores to buy treats such as Сухаріки and морозиво «Львівське», buy small things, and play different games that anyone could imagine such as Хованки, Доганялки. Holidays in the village were special—they were a time when the whole family sat together, shared different stories, and just enjoyed being with each other.

Traveling between the village and the town was also something meaningful to me. It took about an hour by bus, and I made the trip often. The atmosphere was always cozy, even though the bus was crowded with people talking.

In the city, we lived in a small apartment, not far from the center. The city itself was not big—about 20,000 people lived there. I was lucky that my school was close to home, just a five-minute walk away. The school was also small, with about 900 students. In Ukraine, we did not divide schools by grades, so from first grade to twelfth grade, you stayed in the same school. That was normal for us. As a kid, I always looked at high schoolers and wanted to be like them. Now I am like one of them. I now understand high schoolers only study, work, and get little sleep, without much free time to spend.

Everything was good until ninth grade, when the war started. My whole class was shocked. No one knew what was going to happen. My mother immediately started packing our things, and we moved to the village. We stayed there for twelve days. One day, my grandpa learned the Polish border was open to anyone escaping the war. He told us we might want to consider leaving Ukraine and escaping all the chaos. Without hesitation, my mom, my brother, and I went to the local bus station, bought tickets, and traveled to Poland, where we stayed for nine months.

Poland was special for me because it was the first time I experienced things without limitations—like food. It felt more alive than Ukraine at that time, and it made me happy. During those nine months, I struggled with stress from the war. I missed my country so much and wanted to return, but thankfully, my entire family was in Poland, which helped me forget about it a little.

My father has a sister in America who was lucky enough to win a green card lottery; she had been living there for twenty years. The US had a program, "Uniting for Ukraine," which allowed families to reunite if they were in different countries. So, we applied. One night, my mother told me there was a possibility that we would be moving to the US. At that moment, I was scared. I had only seen America in movies like The Terminator. It was hard to believe, and honestly, it felt intimidating.

For the first two days after hearing the news, I could not believe it. Emotionally, I was terrified. A new country meant a new language, a new life—everything unfamiliar. On the day of departure, early in the morning, our family took everything we needed and headed to the capital of Poland to catch our flight. The drive took about two or three hours. The whole time, I was thinking about what my life in America would be like. I tried to cheer myself up somehow, but it was hard.

At the international airport, I saw so many different cultures, people from all over the world. It was overwhelming. We waited for two hours. I was scared of flying, so I was stressed the whole time. But when it was finally time to board, I started feeling calmer because my family was with me.

As the plane took off, I stared out of the small window. It was strange to see how high we were. The whole flight, I did not sleep—I did not want to. Instead, I talked with my brother about how he felt about everything. He said he felt confident.

After twelve hours, we arrived at Chicago O'Hare International Airport. Seeing America for the first time felt like a dream. But I was exhausted. When we landed, the airport guards took us to a room for a check. We sat there for two long hours. I was nervous because we were supposed to meet family members living in the US, but I did not see them. My dad started getting really worried. After what felt like forever, we were finally allowed to leave.

At the entrance of the airport, we met our relatives, who had been waiting for us. They helped us with our bags and packed everything into the car. I did not know most of them—I had never seen or even heard of them before. But my parents knew them well and were surprised at how much they had changed over the years. After loading our things into different cars, my brother and I rode with our cousin. He told us that life here would be different from Ukraine and explained some basic things while we drove to my aunt's house.

When we arrived, I met my aunt for the first time. We had a short conversation—mostly the usual "How have you grown up?" kind of talk—and then I fell asleep. I was completely exhausted. The next day, we woke up, and another cousin drove us to our temporary home. It was a small apartment in a building that housed four different families. It was nice, and it was the first time I really saw what American houses looked like.

Our first time going shopping was surprising. Initially, I thought the prices were much lower than in Ukraine. However, later I realized the value of the currency was different. Things we could not afford before, we could easily buy here, especially imported goods. From excitement, we bought all sorts of things—from clothes to food to electronics.

I started school after two weeks in America. I was afraid because I had to make new friends, and my English was not great. The night before, I could not sleep at all. But when I arrived, everything seemed normal, except for the language difference. When I entered my first class, everyone looked at me. I was so scared I could not even say a word. The teacher placed me in a seat, and eventually, I met my first classmates. We exchanged a few words, and the lessons continued.

I have been here for two years now. I changed schools only once. I started at one school but later transferred to Stevenson High School when my parents found a new apartment. They chose to move so I could get a better education, even if it meant living in a smaller apartment.

At Stevenson, I have made some friends, and I found subjects that I enjoy. I do not have any hobbies yet, but I plan to find one. At home, I follow a daily routine—waking up, going to school, and coming home. I spend time talking to my friends and playing video games together. Sometimes we meet each other and go to each other's houses; we often travel together to famous places in Chicago such as the Chicago History Museum and the Navy Pier, or go on field trips to different skyscrapers. But it does not have the same spirit as it did back home, when I would go outside with my friends after school and walk on the streets of Ternopil.

I am planning to finish school next year, and hopefully to try to help people the same as me who are new to this country and are going to Stevenson. After finishing school, I will be probably going to college here and have a stable future. I also want to help my parents, whether by supporting them financially or just being there for them. They have done so much for me, and I want to do the same for them.

VIDEO LINKS

greencardvoices.org/speakers/matviy-buyarskyy

BUILDER
VISION
SOUTH AMERICA
Lima,
Peru

Andrea Verne

Born: Lima, Peru

"MOVING MEANT GIVING UP A LOT OF THINGS, INCLUDING TRADITIONS AND CELEBRATIONS THAT WERE IMPORTANT TO ME IN PERU."

I was born in Peru, a country in South America. Specifically, I was born in Lima, the capital city, where most of the major activities and events happen. One of the most vibrant districts, Miraflores, is known for its lively streets filled with music, dance, and people socializing both day and night. The daytime is usually pretty. You can walk from one store to another store. There is a park with cats, a very touristy place. In Miraflores, you can go shopping, eat food, and experience everything.

Growing up in Lima, I was very close to my family and friends. I attended a school called Hans Christian Andersen, which was near my house. Sometimes I would walk to school, and other times my dad would drop me off. My mom told me that on my first day of school when I was just three years old, I cried because I was nervous and did not want to go. My teacher had to bring me candy and balloons to calm me down before I finally went into the classroom. That day, I met two friends, and we have remained close ever since.

My family consisted of my mom, my dad, my sister, and our dog. Life in Peru was different from life in the US. One of the things I loved the most was spending time with my extended family. Every Friday, Saturday, or Sunday, we would gather with my cousins and celebrate holidays and special occasions. Being close to my family was natural for me, and it is one of the things I miss most about Peru.

Since I was around seven or eight years old, my parents had mentioned the possibility of moving to the United States. At first, I did not take it seriously. I thought it was just something they said out of excitement, but that would not actually happen. However, as I got older, they kept bringing it up, and by the time I was eleven, the idea became more real.

Getting the necessary documents to move to the US was a difficult process. It took five or six months. During that time, I was not going to school. My dad told me how complicated the process was, so I did not think much about it—until one day, my parents told me that everything was ready and we were officially moving. At first, I did not believe it. I asked them multiple times if it was real, and they confirmed that it was. This was before COVID-19, but because of the pandemic, we had to postpone our plans. We had to wait until the US embassy contacted us again. After a few months, my dad finally received the approval, and that was when I knew for sure that we were moving.

I had mixed feelings about it. On one hand, I was excited about the new opportunities ahead, but on the other hand, I was sad because I realized I would not get to experience my teenage years in Peru. That was something difficult to accept. I would have to leave everything behind.

Before leaving, my dad had to sell our car and many other things in our house. I did not want him to sell the car because I had so many memories attached to it, but eventually, I understood that it was just an object. Letting go of some of my childhood belongings was hard, but I knew it was necessary. After some thinking, the main reason I decided to leave was that my future would be better and more successful in the US than in Peru. In Peru, you do not have many opportunities. It is also not safe—theft and robbery are common, making it an insecure place to live.

My parents chose Chicago as our new home because we had family there, on my dad's side. Many of our relatives from Peru had already moved to Chicago, so my parents wanted to be close to them. That part made me happy, because we had only been able to see them during short trips to the US for holidays or summer vacations.

Moving meant giving up a lot of things, including traditions and celebrations that were important to me in Peru. For example, whenever the national soccer team played, my family would get together to watch the game. Every Christmas, we spent time together. Knowing that I would not experience that in the same way anymore was difficult. More than anything, I was sad that I would not see my cousins grow up alongside me or spend as much time with my grandparents. That was one of the hardest things to accept.

I arrived in the US in July 2021. The first thing I noticed was how different the air smelled—it just felt different. My uncle and aunt picked us up from the airport; as soon as we got into the car, my uncle said, "Welcome to the United States." He told me that we would face challenges, but that they would also be opportunities for growth.

At first, adjusting was tough. I attended middle school for seventh and eighth grade, and to be honest, I did not like it. I did not feel like it was a welcoming space, and I did not have many options to explore new things. But once I started high school at Stevenson, everything changed. I made new friends, and I finally felt like I had more opportunities to participate in different activities. There were so many options—sports, clubs, and events—that made me feel more included and comfortable.

Now, I stay after school to work out in the gym. I also like to study with my friends. During the sports season, I will try out for soccer. I study every day to get good grades and to show my parents that moving here was worth it.

Looking ahead, I want to study marine biology. Ever since I was a kid in Peru, I loved the ocean and spent a lot of time by the water. My goal is to study marine biology in the US, gain knowledge and experience, and then take what I have learned back to Peru and improve it.

VIDEO LINKS

greencardvoices.org/speakers/andrea-verne

PUMA
ASIA
Syria

Nour Khashouk

Born: Syria **Raised:** Lebanon

"I WAS SO SAD. I HAD FRIENDS IN SYRIA. I HAD SOME OF MY COUSINS THERE. I DID NOT WANT TO LEAVE."

In 2007, I was born in Syria. Syria is the Old City. It was good for me. I had friends in Syria. I loved it so much. I used to walk with my friends, play soccer, and go buy some snacks every time. It was so good.

When I was six years old, my parents said, "We need to leave Syria." I was so sad. I had friends in Syria. I had some of my cousins there. I did not want to leave.

I think it was April 1, 2013, when my dad said, "It's time to go. We need to leave Syria and go to another place, Lebanon." I came to Lebanon on April 1, 2013. It was good and became my second home, but some people would say, "Go back to Syria. Go work."

After three years, my dad passed away. I was so sad. I was the only son for my mom. I had to work. I had to go to work and go to school. It was hard, at eleven years old, to do both at the same time.

Still, I kept going to school. For three years, I worked very hard. After that, I had to stop going to school because my mom did not have any work available to her. My mom said sorry, but I did not stop. I kept working for six years.

It was hard for me. I woke up at 7:00 a.m., went to work, and stayed there until six. Then I would see my mom and my cousins. I did not get to see the rest of my family. I worked from eight to six every day, and it did not give me much money—not enough to pay for everything, not enough for the rent, not enough for the bills.

On November 25, 2020, someone called from the United Nations. They said we could go to America. When I came back from work that day, my mom told me, "Someone called me. We might go to the USA so you can continue your education."

I was so sad, but also so happy. I was sad because I did not want to leave my cousins and my friends. But I was happy because I really wanted to continue my education. For seven years, I had been working, and now there was a chance.

After that call, my mom said it would take time. We worked on the papers for one year. Then I came here.

It was sad because I had to leave my cousins, my new friends. It was good because most of my cousins had already left Syria and come to Lebanon. But still, saying goodbye was so hard.

In February 2024, I came to America. My last day in Lebanon was beautiful. I saw my uncle and my cousins. That night, my cousins came over. We had fun, stayed up late, listened to music, and danced. It was my last day in Lebanon.

We took an Uber to the airport. In the Uber, I kept looking at Lebanon, saying goodbye to everything for the last time. I took the airplane and came here. When I arrived, I had a nice welcome. I had not seen my aunt and cousins in fourteen years. I was so excited to say hi again.

The first day was amazing. My cousins made breakfast and showed me new things for my new life. The first week was good. After one month or two months, my aunt took me to see the city and go to the market. But I did not speak English when I came here. It was hard because when someone talked to me, I could not understand anything.

During spring break, I stayed home and practiced English. After one month, the school opened. I started going to school. I saw my cousin at school too. I worked very hard because I wanted to learn English. I wanted to speak with people, to understand everything when they talked to me. I learned English fast because I loved it. I loved school so much. I learned English. I learned another language too. I was so excited for that.

I used to live in Beirut, the capital city. I loved the weather there. I loved the summers and the people.

Right now, I am going to high school. I am a sophomore. I want to make my dream come true. I live with my mom and my grandma. Every weekend, my aunt and my cousins, and I go to different places.

I have friends at school. We play soccer together. In the mornings, I wake up, go to school, and go to work. When I finish work, if I have time, I play soccer or basketball. I love basketball so much. It is good for me.

My dream is to become a mechanical engineer. I work so much to make this a dream.

VIDEO LINKS

greencardvoices.org/speakers/nour-khashouk

MEXICO
SOUTH AMERICA
Mexico

Aranza

Born: Mexico

> "I WANT TO TELL EVERYONE TO NEVER GIVE UP, BECAUSE THERE ARE ALWAYS OPPORTUNITIES."

I was born in Mexico. My family is my father, my mother, one brother, and one sister. My siblings are younger than me. In Mexico, I enjoyed cooking tamales, chilaquiles, spaghetti, milanesas, and pozole.

There were many problems and insecurity. There were always shootings; people were being tortured, beaten, and robbed. My family had a business; one day they were threatened and almost lost their lives. The lack of safety kept getting worse. My family decided to leave because they continued to be threatened.

In February 2024, we moved to America. From Mexico City, we took a plane. We stayed there for one month, waiting for immigration to let us pass. We were living in tents on the border. Finally, an immigration officer called us, and we stayed in a detention center. With a little money, a kind man took us to Phoenix.

When I arrived in Phoenix, my family and I stayed at the airport for three days to collect money. We had to ask for help so that we could board the flights. My mom's friend supported us a little, and there were other people who helped us. When we boarded the flights, my parents, my siblings, and I arrived in Chicago with my aunt. We arrived without money, without anything. We arrived alone. At first, it was very difficult because my parents did not have a job, we did not know anyone, and we did not understand English at all. With time, my parents found stable jobs, thank God. Now we are a little better, and my siblings and I understand English better.

When I arrived in Chicago, I felt sad because I had left everything in Mexico. I also felt angry because of all the insecurities we had to leave. Then I understood we have more opportunities here; it is safer, and I do not have to worry about something happening to my parents. Now, I just hope that I can be in charge and that I can fulfill all my goals, getting what I want so that I can be okay with my family.

In May 2024, I started going to high school. I play sports. I go out with my new friends. I go out with my family, visit places, and sometimes go shopping. I just do not like that I do not see my parents often because they work for many hours.

I want to be a flight attendant. My hopes for myself are that I can make it, to be someone in life. So far, I am doing well at school. I hope I can achieve my goal of being a flight attendant so I can support my parents, because they brought me here to give me a better future. I want to tell everyone to never give up, because there are always opportunities.

VIDEO LINKS

greencardvoices.org/speakers/arzana

Afterword

Learning from the students' stories featured in this book is just the beginning. The more important work starts when we engage in the difficult, essential, and brave conversations about the changing face of our nation.

Immigration plays a significant role in modern America—and our work seeks to build bridges that facilitate rich conversations and understanding. Consider, one in five Americans speak a language other than English at home- what a powerful opportunity for new connections and cultural growth! From classrooms to book clubs, from the individual interested in learning more about his immigrant neighbor to the business owner looking to understand her employees and business partners, this book is an important resource for all Americans.

This collection also includes a selection from our ***Act4Change*** study guide. *Act4Change* is an experiential learning tool promoting further participation among readers through scaffolded and thoughtful discussion questions and activities focused on hands-on learning. Each activity emphasizes personal growth and knowledge acquisition. The goal is to help teachers, students, and those experiencing our multimedia publications to more closely examine their own stories, while learning about the lives of others.

You can also further engage with your communities and learn more about contemporary immigration through ***Story Stitch***, a card-based guided storytelling activity which connects individuals across different backgrounds by encouraging them to share and connect through stories. In addition, the Green Card Voices' travelling ***state or national exhibits***, allow for a visual experience with these and others students' journeys, An interactive presentation, these exhibits feature QR links to students' video narratives designed to expand the impact of published collection of personal narratives of their travels to the United States.

Our aim is to spark deep, meaningful conversations about identity, appreciation of difference, and our shared human experience. To learn more about in-person and virtual speaking events, traveling exhibits, and other ways to engage with the other *Green Card Youth Voices* stories, visit our website: www.greencardvoices.org.

Act4Change

A Green Card Voices Study Guide

Each person has the power to tell their own story in their own voice. The art of storytelling translates across cultures and over time. In order to learn about and appreciate voices other than our own, we must be exposed to and given tools to foster an understanding of a variety of voices. We must be able to view the world from others' perspectives in order to act as agents of change in today's world.

Green Card Youth Voices is comprised of the inspirational stories from a young group of recent immigrants to the US, which they've generously shared with a wide audience. This study guide will provide readers with questions to help them explore universal themes, such as storytelling, immigration, identity, and perspective.

Introduce New Voices:
Participants will select one of the thirty storytellers featured in *Green Card Youth Voices* and adopt that person's story as their own "new voice." For example, one participant may choose Mussa Mrisho while another might choose Andrea Verne. Participants will become familiar with the life story of their "new voice" and develop a personal connection to it. After each participant has chosen his or her "new voice," read the personal essay first and then watch the video.

Act4Change 1:
Answer the following questions—

1. Why did you select the storyteller that you did?
2. What was interesting to you about their story?
3. What do you and the storyteller have in common?
4. What have you learned as a result of reading/listening to this person's story?

Learn About New Voices 1:

Divide participants into groups of three or four people. Provide each group with copies of the written narratives from five selected stories. Each person within each group will read one of the five narratives. Once finished, the participants will share their narratives with the others. Then, as a group, choose one of the five "voices" and watch that person's video.

Afterward, go on to the journal activity below.

Act4Change 2:

Answer the following questions—

1. What new information about immigrants did you learn from this second storyteller?
2. Compare and contrast the storyteller's video to their story. Which did you prefer? Why?
3. What are some similarities between you and the second storyteller?
4. If this really was your "new voice," what might you want to know about America upon arriving?
5. If you could only bring one suitcase on your move to another country, what would you pack in it? Why?

Learn About New Voices 2:

Each participant will be given a third "new voice." Only one can go to each student; there can be no duplicates.

Inform participants not to share the identity of their "new voice." Participants will try to match their classmates' "new voices" to one of the stories in the book. Encourage participants to familiarize themselves with all of the voices featured in *Green Card Youth Voices*.

Act4Change 3:

1. After they are given their "new voice," ask participants to try and create connections between this third voice and themselves. Have the students read their story and then watch the video of their "new voice." Have them think of a piece of art, dance, song, spoken word, comic, sculpture, or other medium of their choosing that best describes their "new voice."
2. Participants will present a 3-5 minute artistic expression for the larger group from the perspective of their "new voice" in thirty-five minutes. The audience will have a template with a chart that includes each of the thirty GCYV students' names, their photo, and a one or two-sentence abbreviated biography. Audience members will use this chart throughout the activities to keep track of what has been learned about each voice that they have heard.
3. Ask the participants to describe the relationship between the *Green Card Youth Voices* and themselves:
    a. What did you notice about the form of artistic expression and the story?
    b. What drew you to this specific art form?
    c. Do you notice any cultural relationships between the "new voice" and the piece of art that was chosen?
    d. What is your best advice to immigrant students on how to succeed in this country? State? City?

More than Meets the Eye:

In small groups, have participants read and watch three or four selected narratives from *Green Card Youth Voices*. After that, have group members tell each other facts about themselves and tell the others in the group what they would not know just by looking at them. For example, participants can share an interesting talent, a unique piece of family history, or a special interest. Then have group members discuss things that they found surprising about the students in *Green Card Youth Voices.*

Think about the "new voice" you transformed in *Act4Change 3*. Tell your group something that was "more than meets the eye" from the perspective of that "new voice!"

For the complete version of *Act4Change: A Green Card Voices Study Guide*, visit our website—www.greencardvoices.org

See also:
Act4Change: A Green Card Youth Voices Study Guide, Workshop for Educators
This workshop is a focused learning experience crafted to deepen teacher understanding and provide instructional strategy, particularly designed to be used in conjunction with *Green Card Youth Voices.*

Glossary

Apostles: the twelve main followers of Jesus in the Christian Bible, chosen to spread his teachings and lead the early church after his death and resurrectionlanguage

Arepa de huevo: a traditional Colombian deep-fried cornmeal cake, crispy outside, soft inside, and stuffed with a whole egg, eaten for breakfast or as a snack

Assimilating: the process of adjusting to and becoming part of a new culture, often by learning the language, customs, and behaviors of that society

Biryani: flavorful rice dish originating in South Asia with basmati rice and marinated meat and/or vegetables with a mix of spices, herbs, and saffron

Bishkek: the capital of Kyrgyzstan that borders Central Asia's Tian Shan range, known for popular attractions such as Ala-Archa Gorge and Osh Bazaar

Buffalo Grove: a village in Illinois, near the big city of Chicago, and within Lake and Cook counties

CBP One: a mobile app by U.S. Customs and Border Protection (CBP) that helps people submit information, schedule appointments, and request legal immigration entry into the US

Chirchiq: the status of being a legal citizen of a country

Coastal town: a small town located near the ocean or sea, larger than a village but smaller than a city

Сухарiки: in Ukrainian, it means dried bread

Detention center: a place where people are held for a short time when they have problems with their immigration papers or are waiting for a decision about staying in a country

Epilepsy: a condition that affects the brain and causes someone to have recurring seizures, which are sudden changes in how their body moves or feels

Expo Ganadera: a big event where farmers show animals, and there's also a small fair with food, music, and fun activities for families

Garrett's popcorn: a famous Chicago-based popcorn shop known for its unique blend of sweet and savory flavors

Green Card Lottery: called the Diversity Immigrant Visa Program, it gives people from countries that don't have many immigrants in the US a chance to get a visa and live in America

ICE: stands for "US Immigration and Customs Enforcement", a US federal agency responsible for enforcing immigration laws and checks who is allowed to stay in the country

Immigrant center: a place where immigrants stay temporarily while they wait for their immigration process to move forward or for legal decisions to be made

Inflation: an increase in the prices of goods, foods, and services in an economy

Insecurities: the state of being vulnerable to a threat when feeling unsafe or unsure about what will happen

IOM organization: a United Nations agency that helps people who are migrating, especially those forced to move due to conflict, disaster, or poverty

Java: a computer language that helps people make games, apps, and websites that can work on different computers

Kasulu: a town in western Tanzania near the border with Burundi, close to several refugee camps including Nyarugusu

Kigoma: a city in western Tanzania near Lake Tanganyika, often known as a transit point for refugees from neighboring countries

Kurta: a loose shirt or tunic that is worn in many regions of South Asia

Kutya: a sweet porridge made from wheat grains, honey, and ground poppy seeds, often with raisins and nuts added

Kyrgyz: refers to people from Kyrgyzstan

Little Village neighborhood: a neighborhood in Chicago called La Villita and celebrated for its Mexican culture

Malaria: a deadly disease spread by mosquitoes, common in parts of Africa, that causes fever, chills, and can be life-threatening without proper medicine

Makazi: the name or title given to the leader of the Kigoma Refugee Camp in Tanzania, who prevented people from leaving and used his power to control and exploit others

Marine biology: the study of life in the ocean and saltwater environments

Mechanical engineer: a person who designs and builds machines, tools, and mechanical systems, often working in industries like transportation, manufacturing, and energy

Miraflores: a district of Lima Province, in Peru. One of Lima's wealthiest districts and south of the downtown area

морозиво «Львівське»: in Ukrainian, an ice cream with vanilla inside and chocolate outside on a stick like a lollipop

Nochebuena: a tradition celebrated on the night before Christmas, where people come together to honor the birth of Jesus with food, music, and love

Nyarugusu: a large refugee camp in Tanzania that has hosted people fleeing conflict from countries like the Democratic Republic of Congo and Burundi

Osh: the second-largest city in Kyrgyzstan within the Fergana Valley, "capital of the south"

Protested: a form of expression or action showing you don't agree with the rule, decision, or something that's happening

Pungsan: just west of Goyang City, which is a town northwest of Seoul, the capital city

Python: a computer programming language that helps people tell computers what to do, like making games, websites, or pictures with data

Rancho: a home in a rural place, often with animals or crops; quite like a farm

Roblox: a game on the computer or tablet where you can play and have fun with friends in different worlds

Rohingya: an Indo-Aryan Ethnic group residing in the Rakhine State of Myanmar though members cannot obtain citizenship; many are refugees—the United Nations considers the Rohingya population as one of the most persecuted minorities in the world

San Miguel El Alto: a small town in Jalisco, Mexico, with a population of 26,000

Sarees: a garment that is a long unstitched piece of fabric draped around the body traditionally worn by women in South Asia

Shortages: a period where basic living items and necessities to survive are not accessible

Squash: a fast-paced sport or game where two players hit a small rubber ball against a wall using rackets, trying to outplay each other in a closed court

Suhak hakwon: a private math academy where kids go after regular school to learn math earlier or get extra help, and it must be paid to attend

Swahili: a widely spoken language in East Africa, especially in countries like Tanzania and Kenya, and used as a common way for people from different ethnic groups to communicate

Syrian Civil War: an ongoing conflict that began in 2011 in Syria, involving the government, rebel groups, and other nations, leading to a major humanitarian crisis and millions of refugees

Tax Law: the set of rules created by a government that explains how individuals and businesses must pay taxes on things such as income, property, and sales

Telegram: an app where people can chat, share photos and videos, and create channels to send messages to anyone

Tepabril: an annual event held in Tepatitlán de Morelos, Jalisco, Mexico, that lasts the full month of April

Terrorist: someone who uses violence or threats to scare people and try to get power or make political changes

Tía: stands for "aunt" in Spanish

TPS: stands for "Temporary Protected Status", a US immigration program that allows people from certain countries to work and live in the US temporarily due to unsafe conditions in their home country

Ulaanbaatar: the capital of Mongolia, known for being the coldest capital city in the world and sits high up on a plateau at an elevation of 4,430 feet above sea level

United Nations: an international organization made up of countries around the world that work together to promote peace, human rights, and solutions to global problems

Xenophobia: when someone is unfair or unkind to people just because they come from a different country

Хованки: in Ukrainian, it means the hide-and-seek game

Yoruba: one of the largest ethnic groups in West Africa, mainly found in Nigeria, with a deep culture, language, and history that includes music, religion, and storytelling

Доганялки: in Ukrainian, it means the game tags

About Green Card Voices

Founded in 2013, Green Card Voices (GCV) is a nonprofit organization that utilizes storytelling to share personal narratives of America's immigrants, establishing a better understanding between the immigrant and their communities. Our dynamic, video-based platform, book collections, traveling exhibits, podcast and *Story Stitch* circles are designed to empower individuals of various backgrounds to acquire authentic first-person perspectives about immigrants' lives, increasing the appreciation of the immigrant experience in America.

Green Card Voices was born from the idea that the broad narrative of current immigrants should be communicated in a way that is true to each immigrant's story. We seek to be a new lens for those in the immigration dialogue and build a bridge between immigrants and nonimmigrants—newcomers and the receiving community—from across the country. We do this by sharing the first hand immigration stories of foreign-born Americans, by helping others to see the "wave of immigrants" as individuals, with interesting stories of family, hard work, and cultural diversity.

To date, the Green Card Voices team has recorded the life stories of over five hundred immigrants coming from more than one hundred and forty different countries. All immigrants that decide to share their story with GCV are asked six open-ended questions. In addition, they are asked to share personal photos of their life in their country of birth and in the US. The video narratives are edited down to five-minute videos filled with personal photographs, an intro, an outro, captions, and background music. These video stories are available on www.greencardvoices.org, and YouTube (free of charge and advertising).

Contact information:

Green Card Voices
Minneapolis, MN
www.greencardvoices.org
612.889.7635

facebook.com/greencardvoices
twitter.com/greencardvoices
instagram.com/greencardvoices
linkedin.com/company/green-card-voices

About the Co-Editors and Editorial Advisor

Julie Vang is a queer Hmong American born and raised in St. Paul, Minnesota. With over fifteen years of experience in community organizing and politics, Julie has worked at the intersection of storytelling, holistic healing, and community development. They hold a bachelor's degree in Family Social Science with a minor in Asian American Studies from the University of Minnesota Twin Cities. Their work has spanned legislative advocacy, pre-trial release support in detention centers, intergenerational healing circles, and co-editing several books. In this book, Julie's role included working closely with each student author, reviewing transcripts, and guiding them through the process of developing their stories into written essays. They also coordinated and supervised teachers, partner organizations, copyeditors, and volunteers, while contributing to editing and promotional work.

Dr. Tea Rozman is a multilingual, first-generation immigrant born in Slovenia, then part of Yugoslavia. She studied in the US on scholarships from the Open Society Institute and NYU, and earned a Ph.D. in cultural history with an emphasis on oral history from the University of Nova Gorica. Tea specializes in gathering and preserving first person narratives, with a deep commitment to centering underrepresented voices. She is the co-founder and current Co-Executive Director of Green Card Voices, where for twelve years she has led numerous editorial and storytelling projects. Through her work with GCV, Tea has held space for and listened to nearly 600 immigrants share their stories. She is a 2021 recipient of the Oral History Association/National Endowment for the Humanities Fellowship and co-chair of the Development Committee of the Oral History Association. Her role in this book ranged from securing funding and building partnerships with schools and organizations to recording the stories and editing.

Isabel Bethke is a Ph.D./J.D. doctoral student at the University of Minnesota, where she explores the powerful intersection of law, literature, and migration. Her interdisciplinary scholarship focuses on refugee and asylum narratives, using legal storytelling as a tool to challenge stereotypes and advocate for more just, compassionate immigration systems. With a background that blends English, law, sociology, political science, and immigration policy, Isabel's work seeks to humanize complex legal frameworks and bring greater visibility to the lived experiences behind legal cases. In this book, Isabel served as the editorial advisor, diligently reviewing the introduction, acknowledgements, and final essays, and providing essential legal and immigration-related editing recommendations.

Immigrant Youth Traveling Exhibits

Twenty students' stories from each city in the Green Card Youth series (Chicago, Minneapolis, St. Paul, Fargo, Madison/Milwaukee, Atlanta, and Upstate New York) are featured in traveling exhibits, available to schools, universities, libraries, and other venues where communities gather. Each exhibit features twenty stories from a particular city, each with a portrait, a 200-word biography, and a quote from each immigrant. A QR code is displayed next to each portrait and can be scanned with a mobile device to watch the digital stories. The following programming can be provided with the exhibit: panel discussions, presentations, and community-building events.

Green Card Voices also coordinates a National Exhibit featuring all six cities. This exhibit is available for rental across the country.

Green Card Voices currently has seven exhibits based on different communities across the Midwest and South. To rent an exhibit, please call us at 612.889.7635 or visit www.greencardvoices.org/programs/traveling-exhibits.

Green Card Youth Voices: Book Readings

Meeting the student authors in-person or virtually helps create a dynamic space in which to engage with these topics firsthand. Book readings are a wonderful opportunity to hear the students share their stories and answer questions about their lived experiences.

To schedule a book reading in your area, please contact us at 612.889.7635 or info@greencardvoices.org.

Order Through Our Distributor

Our books and Story Stitch are distributed in the US & Canada by Consortium Book Sales & Distribution, an Ingram Company.

For orders and customer care in the U.S., contact:

Phone: 866.400.5351
PCI Secure Fax (orders only): 731.424.0988
Email (orders only): ips@ingramcontent.com
Online: ipage.ingramcontent.com
Electronic orders: IPS SAN 6318630

Mail: Ingram Publisher Services
Attn: Customer Care
1 Ingram Blvd., Box 512, La Vergne, TN 37086
Hours: Monday–Friday
8:00 am to 5:00 pm CST

For orders and customer service in Canada, contact:

Phone: 800.663.5714
Email: orders@raincoastbooks.com

For more information, visit www.greencardvoices.org/ingram

INGRAM | Consortium Book Sales & Distribution

Other Series Available

Green Card Youth Voices

- *a Minneapolis High School*
- *a St. Paul High School*
- *a Fargo High School*
- *an Atlanta High School*
- *Madison and Milwaukee High Schools*
- *Upstate New York High Schools*

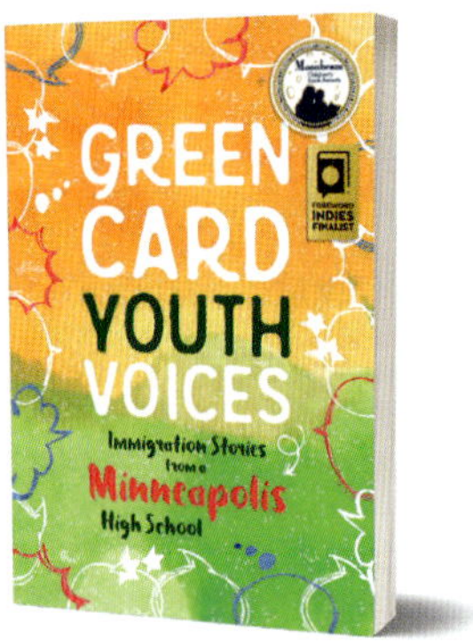

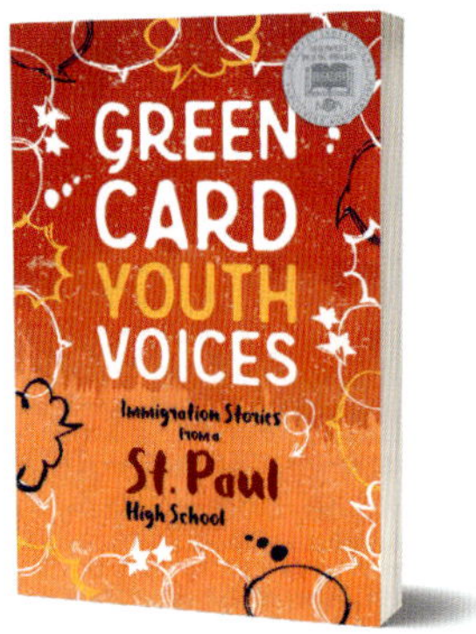

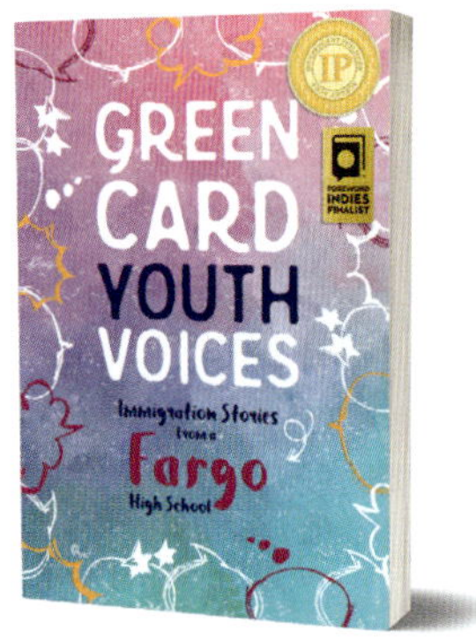

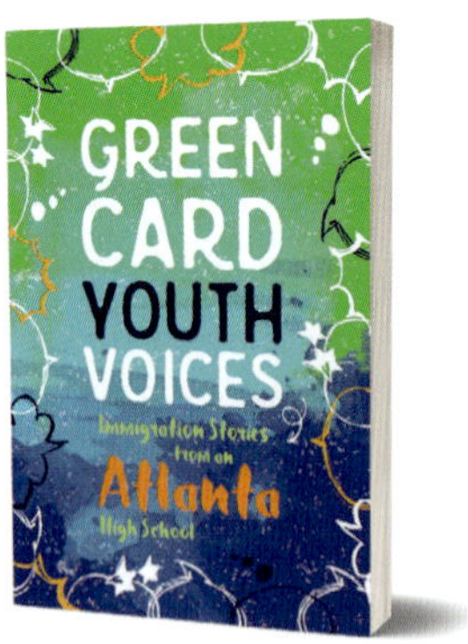

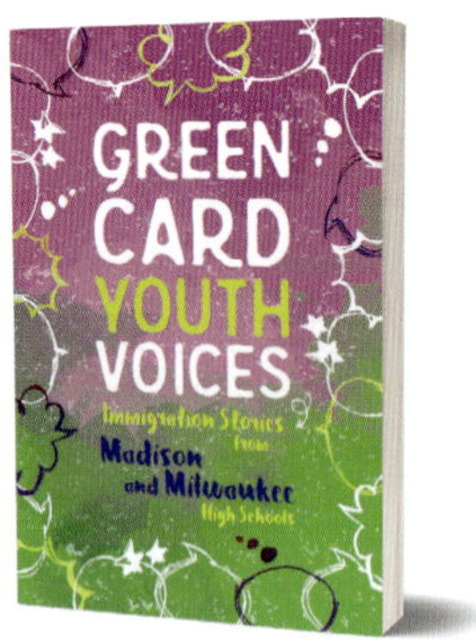

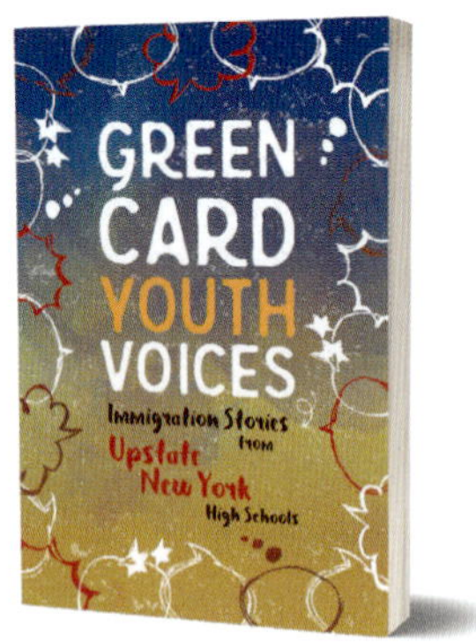

Other Series Available

Bilingual Children's Graphic Novel Series

Powerfully illustrated immigrant stories written in two languages that include discussion questions, important concepts about the stories, and words to know from the stories. Reading comprehension for ages 8+.

Languages available in Spanish, Arabic, Khmer, Hmong, and coming fall of 2025, Ukrainian.

Also Available:

My City Was A Sparkling Jewel:

Voices of Newcomer Youth from Afghanistan

When American troops pulled out of Afghanistan in August 2021 and the Taliban returned to power, the lives of families were radically disrupted. Large, loving, vibrant families that had gone about their daily lives were suddenly separated, and many youth were forced to flee.

Using a trauma-informed approach to storytelling, Green Card Voices and its partners from diasporic Afghanistan, carefully collected first-person accounts of the diverse journeys of nineteen young men and eleven young women on their path to resettling in Minnesota. These stories were gathered at the speed of trust using a mix of handwritten essays and oral storytelling in English, Dari/Farsi, and Pashto.

My City Was a Sparkling Jewel: Voices of Newcomer Youth from Afghanistan shares the challenges faced, opportunities grasped, and dreams these youth had, and still have, for themselves, and for the families and friends they left behind. The storytellers, ages fifteen to twenty, come from various ethnic groups—Pashtun, Hazara, Pashai, Tajik—so their stories detail a wide range of experiences. While the future of Afghanistan and its youth in the United States is still uncertain, these first-person stories illuminate the harrowing contours of the unjust displacement these young people experienced and bear witness to the early days of their resettlement in the United States.

Contents:

- 30 personal essays of Afghan youth living in Minnesota
- 30 full-color portraits/illustrations
- Approx. 200 color pages, 2 maps
- Links to digital audio stories on the Green Card Voices website
- Curriculum
- Glossary

Also Available:

Our Stories Carried Us Here:

A Graphic Novel Anthology

This is a bold and unconventional collection of first-person stories told and illustrated by immigrants and refugees living across the United States. Stanford scientist, deaf student, indigenous activist, Black entrepreneur—all immigrants and refugees—recount journeys from their home countries in ten vibrantly illustrated stories. Faced by unfamiliar vistas, they are welcomed with possibilities, and confronted by challenges and prejudice. Timely, sobering, and insightful, *Our Stories Carried Us Here* acts as a mirror and a light to connect us all with immigrant and refugee experiences. Available as an ebook (ISBN: 978-1-949523-10-2) and hardcover (ISBN: 978-1-949523-17-1).

Contents:

- 10 personal illustrated comics
- Cover by Nate Powell, Graphic novelist/illustrator of *Save it for Later*, *Come Again*, and the John Lewis' graphic memoir, *March*
- Foreword by Thi Bui, Author of *The Best We Could Do*
- Glossary

Also Available:

Green Card Entrepreneur Voices:

How-To Business Stories from Minnesota Immigrants

This is a collection of essays and digital narratives from twenty immigrant and refugee entrepreneurs living in Minnesota. These storytellers come from nineteen different countries. Written in the tellers' own words, these stories offer insight into immigrant entrepreneur expertise: how they did it, why they did it, and what they learned in the process.

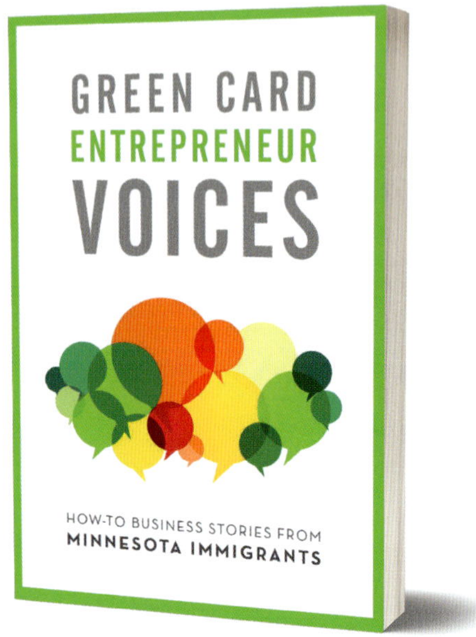

Available as an ebook (ISBN: 978-1-949523-09-6 and paperback (ISBN: 978-1-949523-07-2).

Contents:

- Full color portraits
- 19 personal essays written by Minnesotan entrepreneurs
- Links to digital video stories on the Green Card Voices website
- Forward by Dr. Rajiv Tandon, President of The Institute for Innovators and Entrepreneurs at Hamline University
- Glossary

Also Available:

Green Card STEM Voices:
Stories from Minnesota Immigrants Working in Science, Technology, Engineering, and Math

This is an insightful collection of personal essays written by twenty immigrants and refugees working in STEM and living in Minnesota. Working in seventeen STEM fields and coming from seventeen countries, authors include Raul, a Colombian immigrant who works as a geothermal engineer; Fadumo, a Somali refugee who resettled in Minnesota at age fourteen and invented a portable HIV testing device at her high school; Kim, an immigrant from Cambodia who became the first person in her family to graduate college before pursuing a master's in public health.

Contents:

- 20 personal essays of immigrants working in STEM
- Full-color portraits
- Links to digital stories on the Green Card Voices Website
- Glossary
- 170+ pages

Green Card STEM Voices:
Teaching Guide for Grades 6-12 and College

This unique teaching guide utilizes the perspectives of modern-day immigrants from Africa and Asia. Our diverse storytellers demonstrate the wide range of occupations (chemist, medical researcher, nurse). It is authored by accomplished educators and curriculum developers-including first and second generation immigrants from Africa and Asia – who have added first-hand experiences of the immigration process to each lesson. In line with the National Common Core Standards, these lessons are perfectly suited for grades 6-12, as well as college age. Available on our website at www.greencardvoices.org/store

Also available:

Voices of Immigrant Storytellers:
A Teaching Guide for Middle and High Schools

This ten-lesson curriculum based on the Common Core standards was written and designed by immigrants. The teaching guide progressively unfolds the humanity, diversity, and contributions of new American citizens and situates students' own stories alongside these narratives using eleven Green Card Voices' video narratives. This teaching guide is adaptable for grades 6-12.

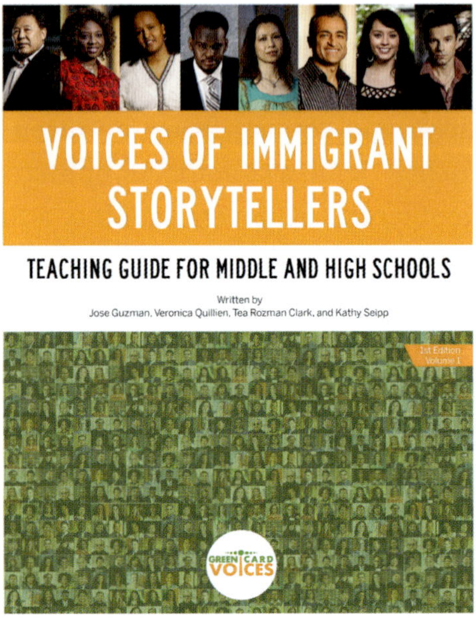

Available as an ebook (ISBN: 978-0-692-51151-0) and paperback (ISBN : 978-0-692572-81-8).

Contents:

- 72 illustrated pages
- 11 Green Card Voices Stories
- 7 ready-to-use worksheets
- 8 classroom activities
- 2 field trip suggestions
- 20 online resources

Now Available:

Story Stitch:

Telling Stories, Opening Minds, Becoming Neighbors

Story Stitch is a guided storytelling card activity that connects and builds empathy between people of different cultural backgrounds. It was created by the diverse Minneapolis / St. Paul community in a series of co-creating game sessions led by the Green Card Voices team. This card game is perfect for: classrooms (ages 10+), diversity training, workshops, workplaces, leadership / fellow retreats, conferences, elderly homes, and more. Available as a deck (ISBN: 978-1-949523-11-9).

Contents:

- 55 full color, laminated cards
- 33 story cards
- 22 stitch cards
- 1 four-sided accordion of instructions

Virtual Story Stitch:

Telling Stories, Opening Minds, Becoming Neighbors

Contents:

- Abbreviated and Extended Story Stitch Questions
- Virtual Instructions Sheet
- Stitch Card PDF and image
- Zoom Technical Troubleshooting
- Informational PDF on Story Stitch

AK
RSITY